# Anxiety 101:

*The Holistic Approach to Managing Your*

*Anxiety & Taking Back Your Life*

By **Eudene Harry, MD**

This book is a work of opinion. Neither the author nor the publisher shall be liable for damages or loss allegedly arising from any information or suggestions contained in this book. While every effort has been made to ensure the information contained in this book is accurate, it is not the purpose of this book to include all information about a healthy wellness program. The author is not rendering professional advice or services to individual readers. The ideas and suggestions in this book do not replace the care and treatment by a licensed medical professional. All matters regarding your health require medical supervision. In addition, information and research are continuously changing, so please understand what is printed here may not be the most current information available.

## Acknowledgements

I want to thank everyone who assisted me on this project; those who inspired me, motivated and at times even carried me. I want to thank my husband who never doubts that I can get anything accomplished even when I am not sure that I can. To my mother, brothers, uncle and his dear wife, thank you for being the best support team in the world. Whenever I need you, your response has always been- just tell us where and when.

This book would not exist if it were not for the groundbreaking work of all the scientist and researches listed in the references and even those who are not. I am constantly awed and inspired by their diligence, intelligence and persistent desire to improve the human condition and help us to live our best life possible. They help me to keep my own fire burning.

# Table of Contents

# Introduction:

*Sound Familiar? Three Case Studies in Anxiety*

Anxiety is a serious concern for millions of Americans and can impact many lives, not just that of the individual suffering with the disorder. For anyone who's suffered with anxiety in any of its forms, or lived with someone – or even known someone – who has suffered, you'll know what I'm talking about.

Its presentation can be severe enough to mimic a serious illness such as heart disease, or mild enough to be passed off as someone who is just "irritable all the time." Either way, for sufferers of anxiety and their friends, spouses, loved ones or even caregivers, they all seek the same thing: relief from anxiety's long-suffering and deleterious effects.

To help illustrate some of the different presentations of anxiety and the possible underlying causes for why people feel so anxious, so often, let's follow three patients on their journey to recovery:

- "**Mary**," who suffers from intense anxiety;

- "**Jennifer**," who for the most part is able to hide her symptoms of anxiety from the world; and

- "**Josh**," who everyone thinks is just plain "cranky."

As you'll soon see, each of these individuals deals with a different level, or degree, of anxiety and yet it takes a foothold in their lives and refuses to let go. That's why treatment and recovery are so important. For now, though, let's meet the patients we'll spend the rest of the book with:

**Case Study # 1:** *Mary*

The first time Mary walked into my office, my immediate impression of her was that she was someone who looked like "a deer caught in the headlights."

To say that she appeared nervous would be a grand understatement. Her hands were shaking and she appeared fidgety. Looking at her chart told me that her heart rate was elevated. She appeared thin and withdrawn and, when she spoke, her words gave off a sense of desperation.

"I feel like I'm jumping out of my skin all the time," she explained, wringing her hands. "I am anxious for no real reason. I don't do the things I used to enjoy. Everything takes so much effort. Just the act of getting out of bed in the morning is so anxiety provoking that I am exhausted for the rest of the day." In addition to these troubling signs, Mary also reported persistent feelings of nausea and a sense of "fullness" in her stomach, especially with the thought of food.

In an effort to eradicate, or at least understand, her symptoms, Mary had already seen her Primary Care Physician, her Cardiologist and her Gastroenterologist. They had all given her a clean bill of health, which was very good, and certainly encouraging, news.

As she was already in her 40s and thought that hormones could be contributing to some of her issues, Mary had also had her hormones evaluated. She was started on hormonal replacement therapy and some herbs for adrenal support that contained panax ginseng.

However, this only served to escalate Mary's anxiety. At that time, she was starting on a sedative medication known as a benzodiazepine to help with her anxiety symptoms, and she stated that she felt like it made a "minimal" difference.

Now, this may seem like more of an extreme case of anxiety, but many of us are walking around with a constant feeling of dread, almost as if we are waiting for "the other shoe to drop." While the act of getting out of bed may not "exhaust" us, who hasn't wanted to lie back down and pull the covers over their head at the thought of facing another anxiety-producing day?

Oftentimes we can relate to Mary's abdominal symptoms, even though it may be at a lesser level. Rather than feeling nauseous, we may instead describe the sensation as "butterflies" or "knots" in our stomachs, or even cramping, making us uninterested in the thought of food or eating.

From time to time, as anxious thoughts bubble to the surface, we may feel a tightness in our chest or the flash of a tension headache. Other times it can feel like just taking a deep breath is real work. Some people experience feelings of palpitations, as if their heart is "skipping a beat."

Many times, like Mary, we cannot specifically identify the source of this anxiety we're feeling, though to us it's very real. Even when we do identify the source, we know that the amount of anxiety we are feeling is out of proportion to the situation at hand. Or, as Mary said when she first presented to me, "I am anxious for no real reason."

In Mary's case, she claimed that she felt like she had always had some underlying anxiety, even as a young person, but it seemed that the escalation of her symptoms coincided with her divorce two years earlier. Since that time she had briefly participated in cognitive therapy work, and had tried an anti-depressant.

Mary reported that the therapy seemed to help the most and she had since stopped the medication because "she did not like the way it made her feel." However, now she felt like everything in her life brought on her anxiety symptoms.

**Case Study # 2:** *Jennifer*

Like Mary, when Jennifer first presented to me she was in her mid-forties. She was married, had two children and a husband and had opened her own business five years earlier. To everyone who knew her, Jennifer appeared calm, confident and self-assured, but she knew differently. To her friends, family, co-workers and customers she presented herself as one thing; but, when alone, she gave in and admitted that she was "merely wearing a mask for the outside world."

Jennifer had gotten to the point where she felt anxiety every day, even with the simplest of tasks. She reported that even checking the mail made her nervous because it may contain "bad news." She went on to say that she could feel her anxiety increase when the phone rang at work because someone may be calling to "chew her out" because an order went wrong. She felt like, no matter how good things were going, she was always waiting for "the other shoe to drop."

Jennifer started a meditation practice, but it became a challenge for her because she said it was often a struggle just to take a deep breath.

"I think I have always been a little nervous," she reported during that first consultation. "But with things I considered normal such as public speaking. Now," she continued, "It seems to be getting worse. I feel like I need to retire and disconnect from everything just so I can live."

Further questioning revealed that Jennifer had suffered from constipation for years. She also shared that there were certain foods that she was convinced made her symptoms of fatigue and anxiety even worse. Energy wise, Jennifer was "wired but tired." She also reported that her cycles seemed to come a little bit earlier and she was starting to experience some hot flashes and night sweats.

**Case Study # 3:** *Josh*

Josh was married with children and owned a successful business. He worked out regularly and considered himself quite fit. He reported that his wife had kept the family on a "health kick" for years.

Josh felt his diet was balanced. He ate primarily organic food, tried to incorporate a variety of vegetables daily and ate only lean meats. Yet, digging deeper, I learned that his cholesterol and blood pressure were elevated and he was on medication for both.

So far, so good; it doesn't sound like Josh had any problems, right? But Josh had presented to me because he had difficulty sleeping and was very easily irritated. "I don't recall the last time I had a good night's sleep," he said, his tone a combination of exasperation and irritation. He further stated that his family and friends were finding it increasingly difficult to cope with his irritability.

When I asked him about the potential source of his anxiety, Jeff stated that he simply felt "overwhelmed" and "worried" about his business, family and children.

"I just feel anxious all the time," was how he put it, echoing the sentiments of both Mary and Jennifer before him, and many of my other patients as well.

## Parting Words about Case Studies in Anxiety

As you can see, anxiety comes in different forms and affects different types of people differently. What's interesting to see is how prevalent anxiety is in modern America and the many ways in which people try to cope with it.

From the descriptions I've provided above, you can see the various approaches used in an attempt to control anxiety, from the natural and even alternative treatments like herbal remedies such as panax ginseng and meditation, to more traditional routes of therapy and prescription medication like Xanax or others.

What works for some won't work for others, and vice versa, but nothing will work if you don't stop in your tracks, recognize the anxiety you feel and pledge to do something about it. Fortunately, that's exactly what this book is about.

# Chapter 1:

## *Anxiety* – *What it is & Why it Exists*

Mary, Josh and Jennifer are just three of the many faces of anxiety. Many of us, like Jennifer, have become extremely skilled at masking our discomfort from the rest of the world. Meanwhile others, like Josh, come across as just plain irritable and maybe even angry, perhaps not even realizing that anxiety is the root cause of their – and everyone else's – discomfort.

Sadly, Mary, Josh and Jennifer are *far* from alone. Statistics tell us that approximately **40 million people** in the United States alone suffer from anxiety with an estimated 15 million suffering with social anxiety disorder.

Unfortunately, less than half of that 40 million – in fact, only about 30% – will seek medical attention, and even fewer will seek out a therapist who specializes in anxiety. Most will visit their primary care physician and probably do so because of the accompanying physical symptoms that accompany anxiety, such as stomach issues, headaches, lack of sleep, etc.

Since anxiety is often so endemic, a "creeping" disease as it's sometimes called, such symptoms can linger for months, even years, before sufferers finally report their symptoms to a general practitioner. And, since initially there is little physical cause for their concerns, patients are likely turned away with little to no relief.

Only when they address the root cause of their physical symptoms, the underlying anxiety that is taking over their lives, will they ever find true relief from what is troubling them, both emotionally and physically.

## The Hidden Cost(s) of Anxiety

As you might imagine, 40 million people is no small change. And the fact is, each of those sufferers from anxiety represent a loss: a loss in productivity, in effectiveness, in relationships, in vibrancy, joy and hope for a better life.

What kind of cost are we talking about here? Well, according to Harvard University, untreated psychological issues such as anxiety will cost the United States an estimated **105 billion dollars** in lost productivity annually. This is due to absenteeism, decreased work performance, increased rates of illness and increased errors as a result of anxiety's deleterious effects.

The occurrence of anxiety has been on the rise over the last 10 years and, with the current concern about the economy and general global unrest, we can only expect this trend to escalate.

Every pink slip, every layoff, every demotion or lost promotion, every single-income household or underwater mortgage or lost value in stocks, bonds and 401(k) programs only increases the amount of anxiety felt by both individuals and, often, their entire families.

Experts believe that another contributing factor in the amount of anxiety Americans feel is our increasing expectations for a "brighter tomorrow," coupled with a perception of decreasing ability to achieve these expectations.

Whenever there is a huge disparity between our dreams and reality, between our perception of what our life "should" be and what it actually *is*, we are prone to experience significant anxiety and distress.

**Breaking it Down:** *Anxiety by the Book*

What, then, *is* anxiety? In simple terms, anxiety is the expression of the signs and symptoms of fear – or the startle response – without an identifiable trigger. In short, you feel almost all the effects of fear without being able to point to the "boogeyman" causing it!

Anxiety may also be triggered by a particular event, but the response may be exaggerated or prolonged in comparison to the event itself. For example, an everyday act such as checking the mailbox evokes a response that is far out of proportion to the act itself. Your respiratory rate increases, your heart starts to pound and your head starts throbbing. It's almost as if you are going to disarm a bomb and you have no idea how to do it, or why you feel this way.

Even when you open the box and find only the mail waiting for you, you are still not able to return to a calm state for quite some time. For many people, these anxious feelings are both random and debilitating. But why do they happen, to whom, and in what way? These are the questions I'll strive to answer in this chapter.

**The 5 Categories of Anxiety**

Anxiety is twice as common in women as it is in men, but no matter who suffers the most, or most often, it can be a debilitating disease for all involved.

Anxiety can be broken down into five distinct categories:

1. **Generalized Anxiety Disorder (GAD)**: This category is marked by excessive worry that you cannot control. Many times there is no identifiable cause or the reaction far outweighs the event. To be diagnosed with this disorder, symptoms must be present for 6 months or longer. Symptoms can worsen around menstruation or during the perimenopausal

period. In men, symptoms can become more pronounced when testosterone levels start significantly decreasing in the mid-forties. Oftentimes, especially in women, GAD (generalized anxiety disorder) is associated with other psychiatric disorders such as depression. Symptoms of GAD include fatigue, irritability, startling easily, difficulty concentrating, nausea, diarrhea, sleep disturbances and muscle tension.

2. **Social Anxiety Disorder or Phobia:** Excessive or unreasonable fear of social situations marks this category of anxiety. It is often accompanied by distorted thinking and constant worrying about being judged or ridiculed by others. It can also be accompanied by physical symptoms such as diarrhea, shaking, upset stomach and palpitations. Just think about the first time you gave a speech to a room full of people. Do you remember the butterflies in your stomach, the nausea or the clammy hands? Then you have experienced social anxiety disorder. Social anxiety disorder (or phobia) is the

most common anxiety disorder and is more common in women than men.

3. **Panic disorder**: This is a more severe form of anxiety and can be very debilitating for those who suffer from it. To diagnose panic disorder, four of the following symptoms are required: palpitations, pounding heart or accelerated heart rate, sweating, trembling or shaking, sensations of shortness of breath or smothering, feeling of choking, chest pain or discomfort, nausea or abdominal distress, feeling dizzy, unsteady, lightheaded, or faint, derealization (feelings of unreality), or depersonalization (being detached from oneself), fear of losing control or going crazy, fear of dying, paresthesias (numbness or tingling sensations) and chills or hot flashes. Symptoms are usually sudden onset and peak after 10 minutes. It may seem to come out of "nowhere." Individuals are usually unable to function at this time and may even feel like they are "dying." Once again, this disorder is more common in women than in men.

4. **Post-Traumatic Stress Disorder (PTSD)**: This extremely serious category is marked by intense fear-based symptoms that develop after witnessing or experiencing a traumatic event that caused or threatened physical harm. Symptoms could include flashbacks, hallucinations, nightmares, and avoidance of anything that triggers memories; as well as hyper-vigilance that could lead to difficulty concentrating, outbursts of anger and irritability, and being easily startled.

5. **Obsessive Compulsive Disorder (OCD)**: Finally, OCD is characterized by unwanted repetitive thoughts and ritualized behaviors that one feels compelled to perform. If one tries to delay or ignore thoughts (i.e., establish control), then this only serves to increase fear and anxiety until one is compelled to perform the ritual to ease anxiety symptoms

While each of these anxiety disorders features its own symptoms, they are most likely to exist on a spectrum and symptoms can oftentimes overlap.

**Why Does Anxiety Exist?**

What can be baffling for most, if not all, of my patients are the following questions:

- *Why does anxiety exist in the first place?*
- *What is its purpose?*
- *Why would the body have a system in place that could potentially make us ill?*
- *And why is it so mysterious, hidden and hard for doctors to diagnose?*

Well, there is actually a very good reason for why the body responds the way it does to anxiety, or stress. You see, once upon a time, back when our ancestors were hunters and gatherers, the anxiety – or stress – response was designed to alert us to potential danger.

Long before cubicles or smart phones, our early ancestors lived in a much more dangerous world where, quite literally, stepping out of the cave each morning could be a life-or-death situation.

Early humans were ever on the alert for danger in the form of wild animals, and even other humans, in a more savage and dangerous world. Therefore, in the presence of danger, this stress response was further designed to give us the ability to move out of harm's way and respond rapidly if needed.

Another aspect of anxiety is that it's designed to keep us alert. As one might imagine, we tend to be more productive when we are alert. Particularly in times of danger, alertness is actually quite a survival instinct. Even in our modern lives, in the absence of hunting and gathering and natural predators, being alert still helps us survive, even thrive, in and out of the workplace.

So, it's not so much that anxiety, or even the full-blown stress response, was ever an unwelcome event in the past. If it saved our lives, after all, we were all for it!

The issue becomes when the stress response is overstimulated and prolonged. When this happens, the constant anxiety can become counterproductive and put us in a state of distress. This exposed state can actually leave us more vulnerable to the very things it was designed to protect us against.

**Fight or Flight:** *The Origins of Anxiety*

To gain a better understanding of how this alarming development can occur, we must first understand the basics of this double-edged sword of protection and potential destruction.

The anxiety response is oftentimes referred to as the "fight or flight" response. That's because the body's reaction is in preparation of one of those two things: fight or flight.

During the fight or flight response, an external event such as a loud or startling noise, a car backfiring or, in our ancestor's case, the roar of a saber-toothed tiger, can trigger the release of the ACTH (adrenocorticotropic hormone), commonly referred to as the "master stress hormone," from the pituitary gland in the brain.

29

This hormone then communicates with the rest of the body, primarily through the adrenal glands. The adrenal glands are small, triangular-shaped organs located on top of the kidneys. When they are stimulated by ACTH, these glands produce several chemicals that play a defining role in the stress response.

Primarily, cortisol and aldosterone are produced from the cortex, or outer layer of the gland, and adrenaline and noradrenaline are produced in the medulla, or center of the gland. So, what do all these hormones do, and how are they involved in making you so anxious, so often?

*Cortisol*

Part of cortisol's function is to increase blood sugar to provide needed energy to muscles and other organs. Think of it as your body's answer to an energy drink right before working out. It does so by increasing the production and release of glucose into the bloodstream. Cortisol is also one of the major anti-inflammatory hormones in the body.

So far, so good, right? This cortisol stuff sounds like it could come in pretty handy. And it does, *if* you're constantly running from danger and trying to survive.

The problem is that most of us aren't Jason Bourne or James Bond, constantly running from the enemy or risking our lives on a daily basis as part of our job description. Instead, we tend to live increasingly sedentary and largely predictable lives. So for us, too much cortisol, too often, can actually be quite harmful.

In excess, for instance, cortisol can increase our risk for diabetes by increasing blood sugar and therefore insulin levels, contribute to weight gain, cause excessive breakdown of muscle tissue and suppress our immune system.

On the other hand, a deficiency of cortisol can leave us more prone to developing allergies, low blood pressure, fatigue and hypoglycemia. So, the balance of cortisol is paramount not only for control of anxiety, but for maintaining optimal health as well.

*Adrenaline*

No doubt you've heard a lot about adrenaline, but what does it actually do and what part does it play in the fight or flight response? Adrenaline acts in the body to initiate a variety of chemical responses which, in turn:

- increase heart rate

- dilate pupils

- decrease motility of intestines (slow down digestion and inhibit bowel movements)

- decrease blood flow to skin and gut in order to provide additional blood flow to large muscles capable of removing us from harm's way

- increase respiratory rate and relax muscles in respiratory tubes to increase oxygen for fuel

All of this prepares us to become alert and ready for potential danger. For instance, dilated pupils allow us to see farther and better, while more oxygen means more fuel, and the ability to run faster, for longer, until we're finally "safe" from whatever threat we're facing.

*Aldosterone*

Aldosterone, the other substance produced by the outer layer of the adrenal glands, helps to maintain normal sodium levels in the body by reabsorbing sodium from the kidneys. Wherever sodium (salt) goes, water follows, so this ultimately has an effect on the blood pressure.

**The Sympathetic and Parasympathetic Nervous Systems:**
*Orchestrating Our Emotions*

As mentioned above, when we are stressed or in an anxiety state, the brain sets into motion a series of reactions that ultimately increase what is known as "the sympathetic response" in our bodies, so called because it arises from the sympathetic nervous system, or SNS.

When the sympathetic nervous system is activated, it stimulates the release of adrenaline and noradrenaline from the adrenal glands. These substances then go on to create several changes in the body.

As we've just discussed, some of the most notable include an increase in heart rate, the slowing of digestion and constricting or narrowing of blood vessels to the gut, skin and distal extremities. During this process, blood vessels supplying the heart could get constricted as well.

Now, the body would not create the ability to have a yang without the ability to create a yin. For example, if activation of the sympathetic nervous system, or SNS, creates excitability, then one would expect a counterbalancing system to create calm once all that "excitement" is finally over. And there is one.

This system is called the parasympathetic nervous system, or PNS. The parasympathetic nervous system, of which the vagus nerve is a big part, has the opposite effect and is the "yin" to the sympathetic system's "yang." Its effects are primarily mediated by the neurotransmitter acetylcholine.

The parasympathetic system can be referred to as the "rest and digest" system as compared to the "fight or flight" nature of the sympathetic system. After the gorging and gushing of blood flow and adrenaline experienced during fight or flight, the PNS decreases heart rate, enhances digestion, urination and motility of the gut.

For a side-by-side comparison of how this chemical "yin and yang" actually work inside the human body, the table on the next page summarizes the functions of the SNS and the PNS:

## How the Autonomic Nervous System Works

| Structure | Sympathetic Stimulation | Parasympathetic Stimulation |
| --- | --- | --- |
| **Iris (eye muscle)** | Pupil dilation | Pupil constriction |
| **Salivary Glands** | Saliva production reduced | Saliva production increased |
| **Oral/Nasal Mucosa** | Mucus production reduced | Mucus production increased |
| **Heart** | Heart rate and force increased | Heart rate and force decreased |
| **Lung** | Bronchial muscle relaxed | Bronchial muscle contracted |
| **Stomach** | Peristalsis reduced | Gastric juice secreted; motility increased |
| **Small Intestine** | Motility reduced | Digestion increased |
| **Large Intestine** | Motility reduced | Secretions and motility increased |
| **Liver** | Increased conversion of glycogen to glucose | |
| **Kidney** | Decreased urine secretion | Increased urine secretion |
| **Adrenal medulla** | Norepinephrine and epinephrine secreted | |
| **Bladder** | Wall relaxed Sphincter closed | Wall contracted Sphincter relaxed |

**Table 1.1:** *The functions of the SNS and the PNS*

## The Autonomic Nervous System, Heart Rate & You

The sympathetic nervous system, the parasympathetic nervous system and the enteric nervous system together are referred to as the autonomic nervous system, or ANS, meaning that its actions are involuntary.

An example of how this system works involuntarily is the heart rate variability (HRV) measurement. The HRV measures the beat-to-beat variability of the heart rate. We may think that having a regular heart beat means that each heart beat occurs at exactly the same time following the preceding beat.

It turns out, however, that a healthy heart actually has a high beat-to-beat variability. A good example of this is the monitoring of fetal, or baby's, heart rate during delivery. The obstetrician would be alerted to the fact that the baby may be in trouble not only if the heart rate drops, but also if it loses the beat-to-beat variability or becomes too steady.

It turns out the same is true for adults. Higher heart rate variability corresponds with better health. What does all of this have to do with stress and, even more personally, your issues with anxiety? Well, it just so happens that people with anxiety disorders and depression have been shown to have lower heart rate variability.

Individuals with low heart rate variability are also at risk for heart disease. According to *Circulation*, the American Heart Association Journal, low heart variability indicates excessive sympathetic tone with reduced parasympathetic tone and can increase our risk for deadly heart rhythms. In other words, the excitatory "flight or fight" response is over activated and the calming "rest and digest system" is on extended standby.

**Are You "Anxious For No Reason?" If So, You're Not Alone...**

The result is that you are left feeling like you are in constant overdrive. Does this sound familiar to you? Are you currently nodding your head? Well, you're not alone. Many of my clients present by saying, "I just feel on edge all the time."

When I press them to be more specific, what they tell me sounds a lot like what I've just described above: they feel "anxious for no reason," their nerves are frayed, they're always on the lookout for "the other shoe to drop," and they are slightly energized even though they're exhausted from being constantly energized!

Several devices are becoming available that are touted to help us identify autonomic nervous system dysfunction through estimation of heart rate variability. Some of these devices are also designed to help train the individual on gaining some control over the "involuntary" autonomic nervous system.

Studies on yogis and experienced meditators have shown that it is possible to have a conscious effect on the otherwise unconscious, or involuntary, autonomic nervous system and thus reduce functions such as heart rate and blood pressure.

A company named "Heart Math" has actually developed several biofeedback devices that utilize heart-centered guided relaxation, while measuring heart rate variability, to determine effectiveness of feedback.

## Generalized Anxiety Disorder (GAD)

Let's take a moment now to look at the dysfunction that occurs in the body with prolonged or inappropriate activation of the stress, or fight or flight, response system. We will be looking at this response and how it pertains to what's known as Generalized Anxiety Disorder, or GAD.

GAD can encompass specific phobias, such as heights, social interaction, etc., or it can be a general feeling of dread without an identifiable cause (i.e., "anxious for no reason"). As we've seen, anxiety isn't just a mental or emotional disturbance, but it seriously and legitimately affects your body in a variety of physical ways.

Constantly flooding your body with cortisol and adrenaline and the responding physical reactions that follow, such as increased heart rate, altered blood flow, etc., can't be good for you. In fact, studies show that high anxiety can increase risk for coronary heart disease and sudden cardiac death in both men and women.

This is especially true for panic disorders. Anxiety is not only physically and socially debilitating, it can have an adverse effect on memory, make us more prone to mistakes and generally make us less productive.

Imagine not being able to get through your everyday routine because it makes you too anxious. Imagine not sleeping well because you are constantly worrying about what's going to happen. It would be like being on red alert all the time.

How exhausted would you be? Well, it's likely that you already know the answer to that question because if you're reading this book, you're probably already anxious and hoping to find some relief.

Let's start by focusing on the causes of anxiety.

# Chapter 2:

## *What Causes Anxiety?*

There are several theories as to what increases one's risk for anxiety, and before we dig too deeply into why anxiety might be plaguing you, I think it's important to dig deeper into a few of these root causes.

**Genetics Play Their Part**

First, there seems to be a genetic predisposition toward anxiety. According to the Mayo Clinic, one's risk of suffering from an anxiety disorder increases if parents or siblings also suffer from the disorder. So, take a magnifying glass to your family tree and then ask yourself:

- *Was one of your parents a worrier?*
- *Is one of your siblings a big worrier?*
- *Is there an uncle or aunt who always fretted and perhaps sought help for his or her affliction?*

The answers to these questions could help you root out why you, too, suffer from anxiety issues. Also, as I've mentioned previously, women are more prone to anxiety. In fact, they are about twice as likely to develop an anxiety disorder when compared to males.

## Anxious Children Can Become Anxious Adults

How far back do the feelings of anxiety, stress and worry go? Have you always been a worrier? Were you anxious as a child? If so, you're not alone. Anxiety that presents itself in childhood is shockingly common and, in fact, it is estimated that some three to five percent of children exhibit some form of anxiety behavior.

This link between anxious children and anxious adults is both strong and pervasive. Studies suggest that children who are worriers – and particularly those who do not like change – are more at risk for developing anxiety issues later on in life.

Research has confirmed that conditions can influence changes in the brain development as early as the perinatal (i.e., the period shortly before and after birth) period. What's important about these findings is that these perinatal changes can make the fear center of the brain more hypersensitive, thereby increasing the risk of anxiety disorders as the child matures.

In support of genetic theory, several genes have already been identified that may play a significant role in the development of anxiety disorders. For example, there is a gene called the RORA (retinoid-related orphan receptor alpha) gene.

This gene's primary function seems to be to protect the brain. This research is extremely significant because variants of this gene have been associated with increased risk of one of the more extreme anxiety disorders: posttraumatic stress disorder, or PTSD.

Variants of another gene called BDNF (brain derived neurotropic factor, i.e., another brain protective chemical) have been shown to be associated with a greater fear response to an incoming stressor in the brain.

Other traditional contributors to anxiety are family dynamics, social isolation and traumatic events or major life stressors. Of course, none of these factors necessarily mean that you *will* develop an anxiety disorder if you experience them. In fact, many people who do go on to lead, for the most part, anxiety-free lives.

## The Body, the Brain & Anxiety

We have identified some of the situations and life circumstances that predispose us to anxiety, but to actively *treat* anxiety we must also have some understanding of what is going on in the body and the brain.

While we have not yet completely uncovered the full mechanism of action involved in the anxiety pathology, the brilliant researchers and scientists laboring to put it all together have instead given us a significant amount of information to parse. Specifically, that information will help us begin to understand and treat this complex disorder while also minimizing the risk of side effects.

This is especially important in today's world, when the concerns about addiction and substance abuse are at an all-time high. Many times patients want a "pill for every ill," and those who suffer from anxiety are no different. But it's important that we learn the root causes behind a patient's anxiety in order to form both a proper diagnosis and treatment regimen.

Having a "one size fits all" mentality when it comes to the prescription pad can be ineffective at best, and potentially exacerbate symptoms at worst. No two sufferers of anxiety are ever exactly the same, even if they suffer from the same disorder and present with the same symptoms. Therefore, we can't apply a template prescription for all our patients.

Age, size, severity of the disorder, other drugs that might interact with our prescription, etc., are some factors that need to be taken into account before suggesting a treatment regimen.

This is especially important when we know the elderly are not only at an increased risk for anxiety disorder, but they are also at increased risk for dementia from one of the most commonly used class of medications for anxiety: benzodiazepines.

**The B.I.G. Mediators of the Anxiety Response**

The major systems that seem to play the biggest role in generating and perpetuating the anxiety response are the **Brain** or neuroendocrine system (including hormones), the **Immune** system and the **Gut.** I commonly refer to this as the **B.I.G. System.**

After our previous discussion, it won't be surprising for you to learn that the brain plays a significant role in the anxiety response. In fact, so prevalent is the brain in causing anxiety that it is often the first line of defense in treating anxiety disorders.

Specifically, it is the target of most first-line anti-anxiety treatments such as Xanax and anti-depressants such as the selective serotonin reuptake inhibitors (SSRI), and more recently, neurofeedback or entrainment techniques. The commonly used medications mentioned above are designed to affect the neurotransmitters GABA and serotonin respectively; as both of these chemicals promote a relaxation response. Neurofeedback and entrainment techniques are thought to work by retraining the brain using brainwave patterns. (This will be explored later in the book.)

The system that may give us pause as being involved in the anxiety response is the immune system. After all, how can the same system that prevents colds and helps us heal minor scrapes and bruises contribute to, let alone prevent, the anxiety response?

However, multiple studies show that this system can and is an important instigator of the anxiety response. It can directly and indirectly affect the other two systems, the brain and the gut, in many cases causing them to upregulate the anxiety response. This occurs primarily through pro-inflammatory chemicals known as cytokines.

The gut, or the "gastrointestinal system" if you're looking for its proper terminology, has also been shown to play a significant role in the anxiety response. Believe it or not, the gut produces many of the same neurotransmitters as the brain, including serotonin and GABA.

The gut also contains about two-thirds of the body's immune system and communicates directly with the brain via the vagus nerve. "Vagus" is Latin for "wandering," which refers to this nerve's long and wandering path from the brain to the gut, connecting to the heart, lungs and voice box (larynx) along the way.

In addition to "wandering," the vagus nerve is commonly referred to as the "calming nerve" in the body. It reduces heart rate, helps to maintain digestive function and even assists with swallowing. As one might imagine, anxiety can affect the function of the vagus nerve.

You can remember these intimate connections inside the body by thinking of the "lump in your throat" and the "pounding of your heart" and the "butterflies in your stomach" symptoms you feel when you experience anxiety (because the vagus nerve is underfunctioning).

The truth is, diagnosed or not, many of us suffer from anxiety or stress on some level. As a result of these symptoms, real or imagined, many people are unknowingly self-medicating with food, alcohol and other illicit or prescribed drugs in an attempt to feel "normal" and be able to function on a daily basis.

Added to this is the fact that certain anti-anxiety medications have been linked to increased risk of dementia in the elderly.

Together, this makes it imperative that we attempt to explore integrative holistic solutions to a very complex issue.

**Revisiting Mary:** *Starting from Scratch*

When I explained to Mary that all these systems could potentially be involved in fueling the anxiety she was feeling, she immediately expressed relief. In particular, Mary felt relieved to know that her gastrointestinal symptoms might not all be her imagination. I could almost see the light bulb going on inside her head as she visibly relaxed in the chair across from me.

Hopefully, she asked, "Do you mean the butterflies in my stomach, the lump in my throat and my heart racing may all be connected?"

When I said that indeed they could be, she was eager to begin. "Let's get on with these tests then," she insisted.

"First," I instructed her, "we need to stop any supplements with stimulants such as panax ginseng, as they may be exacerbating your anxiety symptoms." She readily agreed to do so.

For Mary, we were going to have to "start from scratch" and get her to an emotional and physical "baseline," without stimulants or depressants, to see how severe her disorder might be in order to diagnose her properly and get her on a regimen that was both personalized *and* effective.

# Chapter 3:
## *Anxiety and the Brain*

So, we've seen what happens to the body during times of stress, but now we come to an equally critical question: What is occurring in the *brain* during the anxiety response?

As you might imagine, the answer to this question is extremely complex. That's because many parts of the brain interact with each other simultaneously, creating a kind of "emotional symphony" played by a variety of important chemicals, impulses and reactions.

**Your Brain on Anxiety:** *A Step-by-Step Guide*

In an attempt to simplify the quite complicated process and provide a basic understanding of how the anxiety response occurs in the brain, I will present it as a series of sequential events:

*The Trigger*

At the very beginning of the anxiety response, indeed, to kick off the anxiety you eventually feel, there is an external event, or "trigger." It may be, as we discussed, something physical like checking the mail, something you witness like a traffic accident or something emotional like being called into your boss's office.

Whatever the cause, this input comes into a sensory part of the brain known as the thalamus. From there, the information flows simultaneously through two parallel routes.

One route is designed to generate a quick emotional response and goes through the amygdala, or the "fear center" of the brain. As you'll recall from our discussion of the "fight or flight" response, this allows for a quick reflexive reaction needed to remove oneself from potential danger.

The other route takes a longer path through the intellectual part of the brain, known as the prefrontal cortex, and this allows us to make an executive decision as to the actual danger posed by this event. You might recall experiencing this half of the response when you freeze before opening the mailbox and think to yourself, "Come on, you should quit being such a wimp! What's the worst that can happen?" It's the moment, in fact, where you decide to fight OR take flight.

The fast response route is mediated by the amygdala and is thought to be the reaction primarily responsible for the development of an anxiety disorder. The amygdala is the structure in the brain associated with fear learning and reflexive responses such as a "startle" response.

To prove that the amygdala played a central role in developing generalized anxiety disorder, researchers performed functional MRI studies on the brains of anxious children and compared them to brains of children who did not suffer from anxiety. Both groups were shown a series of "scary" faces. The children who suffered from anxiety showed excessive activity in the amygdala region of the brain.

Another study was performed in adults to see if anticipation of an event would create the same increase in reactivity of the amygdala as the event itself. The results confirmed that the anticipation of the event also caused the same excessive activity in the amygdala as if they were actually experiencing the event itself.

The takeaway from this experiment is that, clearly, worrying about an event can create just as much anxiety as if you were **actually experiencing the event**. If you've ever spent a few days tossing and turning and biting your nails – or even losing sleep – over a trip to the dentist, you'll see the results of this research in your own life.

Speaking of losing sleep, studies using functional MRI to look at this part of the brain during sleep deprivation revealed that a lack of sleep caused a dysfunction in the emotional part of the brain. So, the insomnia created by anxiety can, in turn, worsen the symptoms of anxiety.

Outside of the lab, we often see this self-fulfilling prophecy come true in our own lives. You worry, so you can't sleep, then you worry that you *can't* sleep, and on and on it goes until you get little to NO sleep.

*The Temporal Lobe*

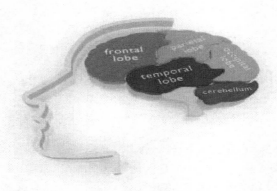

The amygdala is located in the temporal lobe of the brain, one of four major lobes of the brain. The temporal lobe is associated with speech production, memory formation and association, and sensory and auditory processing. The neurons, or the nerve cells, within the amygdala have specialized receptors called N-methyl D-aspartate (NMDA) receptors.

These receptors play an important role in memory formation. As a result, they get activated whether you are learning a response to a fear-inducing stimulus or learning how to respond differently to the same stimulus. The unlearning of a fear response – something I spend a lot of time on with my patients – is often referred to as "fear extinction."

These NMDA (N-methyl D-aspartate) receptors are present not only in the amygdala, but also in other parts of the brain as well. Stimulation of these receptors is an important part of the learning process, but overstimulation of these receptors can escalate the anxiety response and can be extremely toxic to the neurons.

The challenge in dealing with anxiety, be it in our daily lives or even when it manifests itself in a disorder or even phobia, is in striking the right balance between stimulation and overstimulation of these vital receptors.

*The Locus Coeruleus*

Continuing on with our chronology of the anxiety response in the brain, the signal then travels from the amygdala to the locus coeruleus, which is located in the brainstem. The locus coeruleus is the primary area in the brain that is responsible for the production of the neurotransmitter norepinephrine.

Norepinephrine facilitates and modulates behavioral responses to stress. In other words, it makes it easier to take the actions necessary to avoid potential danger. When the locus coeruleus is activated, its primary function is to promote arousal, as we saw with the various physical responses to anxiety – i.e., fight or flight – in the body. As one might imagine, the locus coeruleus is quiet during REM sleep.

During normal arousal, the locus coeruleus is said to be in the phasic state. This means that there is a consistent low level of activity. Think of it as background music at a dinner party. It's on and, if you pay attention to it, you can hear it, but mostly you want to concentrate on what's really important: your guests.

If something new is introduced then the activity level in the locus coeruleus will increase briefly (i.e., the volume gets turned up), thereby allowing the individual to shift focus and attention onto the incoming stimulus. However, in a state of persistent stress or anxiety, the locus coeruleus enters into what is referred to as the "tonic state."

This means that there is a persistent high level of firing or activity in the area, and if there is an introduction of a new situation there is minimal change in activity, since it is already close to peak activation. In other words, if you are attempting to focus on *everything*, it becomes difficult to focus on *anything*.

It's a little like trying to hold a conversation in the middle of a rock concert. In this state, more errors are made and the person is more easily distracted and it becomes difficult to determine what is important.

If you've ever been anxious for an extended period of time – and chances are if you're reading this you're more than familiar with this feeling – you know how difficult it is to "quiet those internal noises" and concentrate on anything for very long. This is one of the consequences of overstimulation during this critical phase of the anxiety response.

## The Hypothalamus

In the next step of the anxiety response in the brain, the locus coeruleus releases large amounts of norepinephrine into other areas of the brain such as the prefrontal cortex (decision-making cortex) and the hypothalamus.

You will hear a lot about this part of the process in the book, because the hypothalamus is the part of the brain that ultimately controls the release of the master hormone, which controls the release of stress hormones from the adrenal glands in the body.

This pathway from the hypothalamus to the adrenal glands is referred to as the hypothalamic pituitary adrenal (HPA) axis. Stimulation of the hypothalamus causes the release of corticotropin releasing hormone (CRH).

Consider this hormone the president, founder and CEO of the company known as Anxiety, Inc. In other words, CRH orders the pituitary gland to respond to the stressful event the same way a CEO orders his or her employees to perform a particular task or meet a specific deadline.

And, just like any good manager, the pituitary then delegates authority. It thinks to itself, "I am all the way up here in the brain so I am going to send a messenger to the adrenal glands so they can carry out the order for me."

The adrenocorticotropic hormone (ACTH) is the messenger from the pituitary that travels to the adrenals to relay the message. Like production employees working in a factory, the adrenals then respond by making the stress hormones cortisol and adrenaline.

Both of these substances contribute toward the stress response by increasing heart rate and blood sugar levels, decreasing blood flow to the intestines and the skin, dilating the pupils, increasing respiratory rate (faster breathing) and creating that general feeling of anxiety.

Like anything else during the anxiety response, less is more and too much is sometimes *way* too much. In this instance, prolonged exposure to these substances in both the body and the brain can lead to trouble with memory, depressed immune system, increased risk for chronic illnesses such as diabetes and heart disease, as well as increased risk for anxiety disorders and depression. This is one more reason to get a handle on your anxiety – particularly your anxiety disorder – before it starts affecting your body as well as your brain.

## Summarizing the Anxiety Response

To summarize this complicated internal process in a much more simplified way, the hypothalamic pituitary adrenal axis is a life saver if you are in trouble and need to remove yourself from immediate danger. However, if left turned on and unchecked, it can flood your system and cause it to malfunction.

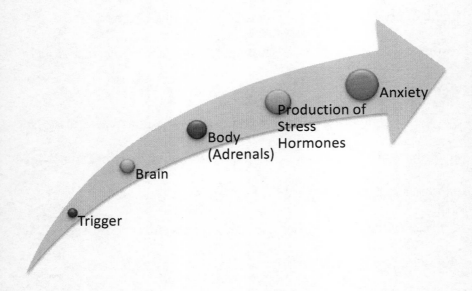

**Figure 3.1:** *From trigger to anxiety – in chronological order.*

When norepinephrine from the locus coeruleus activates the prefrontal lobes, it enhances the ability to shift focus to a new task.

Studies tell us that if moderate or normal levels of norepinephrine are present in the system, then this enhances the attention and memory function of the prefrontal lobes.

However, if levels are significantly elevated and prolonged such as during the stress response, then it can have the opposite of the intended effect and actually impair the ability to focus. This is thought to occur because, depending on the amount of norepinephrine released, different receptors are stimulated in the prefrontal lobes, thereby creating a different reaction with the same substance.

Studies also show that lack of norepinephrine also impairs the ability to focus and concentrate. So, as you can infer, once again it is all about balance.

**Neurotransmitters and the Brain**

Neurotransmitters are messengers the nerve cells use to communicate with each other and bring about action. Think of them as phone lines from one nerve cell to the other. Neurotransmitters are generally divided into two categories:

1.) **Excitatory:** Those neurotransmitters that "rev us up" are often referred to as **excitatory**. They play an important role in keeping us alert and focused, and even have a significant role in memory. Excess levels tend to produce anxiety symptoms and deficiencies can leave us scattered, depressed and forgetful.

2.) **Inhibitory:** The other category of neurotransmitters is often referred to as **inhibitory**. They help to calm us down and give us a sense of satisfaction. Excess levels of inhibitory neurotransmitters can leave us feeling slower than usual, while a deficiency can lead to anxiety symptoms and depression.

To use the car analogy again, excitatory neurotransmitters act like the accelerator – pushing on the gas when we need to get up and go – and inhibitory neurotransmitters represent the brakes, which can come in handy when we need to slow things down. And, just like in a real car, the body's "brakes" almost always wear out and need replacement before the accelerator.

The same is true for our neurotransmitters. If we live in a constant state of "overdrive," always on high alert, anxious and on edge, and repeatedly have to be pulled back or calmed down by our calming neurotransmitters, then it stands to reason that they will need to be replaced first.

As there are different areas in the brain that play a role in the anxiety response, there are also different neurotransmitters that play a role in producing stress as well. Once again, neurotransmitters are chemical messengers in the brain that carry information from one nerve cell to another and, just like any good "conversation," each one has a special message to relay.

We have already (briefly) seen the role of one neurotransmitter, norepinephrine, and how it contributes to fear and stress. Other transmitters thought to play a role in the anxiety response include serotonin, GABA (gamma aminobutyric acid) and glutamate.

I feel it is important to get a brief idea of the role of these crucial neurotransmitters so we can understand the best approach to treating anxiety.

## Serotonin

Serotonin is one of the brain's inhibitory neurotransmitters (think "hitting the brakes"). Interestingly enough, about 90 percent of serotonin in the body is found in the gut (intestines) and only about 10 percent can be found in the brain.

Many of the other neurotransmitters involved in anxiety are also found in the gut, clearly suggesting a strong gut-brain interaction. (But then, if you've ever come down with a severe case of "butterflies" in your stomach during times of stress, uncertainty or anxiety, I'm not telling you anything new.)

Serotonin can promote feelings of calmness, serenity and satisfaction and can help to control your appetite as well. It is made from the essential amino acid tryptophan, found in proteins. Amino acids are the final breakdown products of protein after it has been digested, and "essential" means that it must be obtained from the diet (or from a supplement), as the body is unable to make it on its own.

Serotonin is responsible for a variety of "chain reactions" in the brain, many of which include other neurotransmitters, melatonin levels (affecting sleep) and even our level of inflammation. Case in point: studies show that low tryptophan levels correlate with elevated anxiety levels. The metabolism of tryptophan occurs via two main pathways:

1.) One pathway produces serotonin, which is then converted into melatonin, the substance that helps us sleep at night.

2.) The other pathway creates potentially inflammatory compounds that cross over into the brain and can over-stimulate neuronal activity instead of calming us down.

This increased activity can then promote anxiety, which is counteractive to the usual effects of serotonin. Several other factors, such as high cortisol levels and increased levels of inflammation, can favor the production of these compounds over the formation of serotonin, thus swinging the pendulum toward anxiety. Therefore, we can see that one way stress, infections and inflammation can make anxiety worse is by influencing the metabolism of the amino acid that helps us to make the calming neurotransmitter, serotonin.

When it comes to serotonin, balance is, again, key to building a stress-free life. That's because studies show that low serotonin levels in the prefrontal lobe of the brain can contribute to anxiety. However, excess serotonin has been shown to increase anxiety as well.

We often hear a lot about serotonin on the news or in the doctor's office, but beware of self-prescribing with over-the-counter products promising relief through serotonin. The overdose of supplements or medicines designed to increase serotonin levels can lead to an excess of serotonin, and the constellation of symptoms referred to as "serotonin syndrome."

Mild cases can resemble anxiety and present with increased heart rate, agitation and diarrhea. In severe cases, these symptoms can be accompanied with high blood pressure, dilated pupils, muscle twitching, sweating and headaches. As you can see, this is far from calming. Remember, it's about balance.

## GABA

GABA (gamma aminobutyric acid) is the main inhibitory or calming neurotransmitter in the brain. Like serotonin, GABA is found in the gut as well and has its roots in amino acids. Specifically, GABA is indirectly formed from the essential amino acid glutamine.

Again, essential amino acids can only be obtained through the foods you eat, and now we can begin to see more clearly why a balanced diet is an important part of any program to create a balanced mind. Glutamine is converted to the excitatory neurotransmitter glutamate, which is then converted to the calming neurotransmitter GABA.

Isn't the body amazing, taking something that can potentially cause anxiety and turning it into something that creates calm? The enzyme glutamic acid decarboxylase (GAD) is responsible for this amazing conversion. Therefore, anything that interferes with this enzyme can slow down the formation of GABA and thus cause anxiety symptoms.

For example, vitamin B6 is an important enzyme that increases the efficiency of GAD. A deficiency in vitamin B6 can sometimes manifest as anxiety or irritability, once again highlighting the need to incorporate dietary changes as part of any program targeting anxiety.

An extreme example of the importance of this enzyme in the formation of GABA can be seen in the overdose of the TB drug Isoniazid. This drug can inhibit or interfere with the function of the GAD enzyme, which can then lead to overexcitation of the brain and protracted seizures. Interestingly enough, this form of seizure is treated with large infusions of… vitamin B6!

As you can see, GABA is very important for keeping balance in the brain as a whole. In reference to anxiety, one way that GABA works is by attaching to special receptors (GABA-A) on the neurons in the amygdala (fear center of the brain) to promote a sense of calm.

Deficiency of these receptors in the brain can lead to anxiety symptoms. Researchers have also shown that the activation of these GABA- A receptors in the hypothalamus decreases the production of the CEO hormone (corticotropin releasing hormone), ultimately decreasing the levels of stress hormones in the body. Here again we see that one substance can have multiple effects and that, as ever, balance is critical in controlling, even avoiding, anxiety issues.

**Glutamate**

Glutamate is the most abundant excitatory neurotransmitter in the brain. While we do not yet fully understand how glutamate works, scientists and researchers have started to give us significant insight into the role of this unique neurotransmitter and how it can potentially contribute to the anxiety response. As mentioned above, glutamate is converted from the essential amino acid "glutamine."

Both learning and memory are partially dependent on glutamate's role in activating specialized receptors called NMDA (N-methyl d-aspartate). When activated, these receptors open special channels that allow the influx of calcium into the cells, or neurons. This then leads to signals being transmitted to the nucleus of the cell (it's "brain"), that then causes activation of certain genes to start making proteins that help with memory.

Again, recent studies reveal the "yin and yang" nature of how glutamate acts in the brain and the body. It seems that overstimulation of the NMDA receptors can lead not only to anxiety, but to the injury, and even death, of nerve cells.

On the other hand, a deficiency of glutamate or decreased activation of the NMDA receptors can lead to poor memory formation and retention. So, how does one accumulate too much, or too little, glutamate? There are actually several mechanisms by which this troubling development can occur.

One way that glutamate levels can become excessive is by a dysfunction in the glial cells that surround the neurons. One of the functions of these specialized cells is to remove excess glutamate from the spaces in between the nerve cells (cleanup crew). Any dysfunction in these cells can lead to the accumulation of glutamate that, once again, can overstimulate neurons, thus leading to irritability or anxiety.

Remember the GAD enzyme that converts glutamate to GABA (calming)? Well, a malfunction of this enzyme can also lead to increased glutamate in the system, and therefore increase anxiety. Just remember that glutamate and NDMA receptors aren't necessarily "bad." After all, they play an important role in memory and learning. However, "bad" things can happen to us when there is too much or too little of them in our systems. Once again, it should bring to mind the Goldilocks analogy, not too much and not too little, but just the right amount of activation. In other words, in all things... balance.

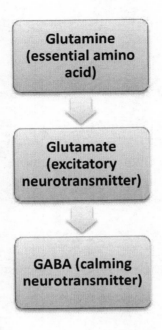

**Figure 3.2:** *Seeking balance in activating neurotransmitters.*

### Norepinephrine

Norepinephrine is another neurotransmitter that plays a role in how well you stay focused throughout the day and, when present in excess, can contribute to anxiety. It is made from the essential amino acid tyrosine. Norepinephrine is also known as noradrenaline.

Its role in the stress response is to help determine the action taken in response to the stressor. Studies show that both actively attempting to get away from an unpleasant stimulus and passively avoiding it by decreasing exploratory behavior due to fear are both mediated by norepinephrine.

For instance, with the right amount of norepinephrine in your system, you can clearly focus and choose between fight or flight, and even what to do in either context. With too much or too little, however, your judgment can become cloudy.

Norepinephrine can also activate the HPA axis that ultimately results in the production of stress hormones. In balanced amounts, norepinephrine acts on the prefrontal lobes to enhance focus and working memory through specialized receptors called alpha 2 receptors. In excess, it seems to affect different receptors that actually can impair memory and focus, rather than enhance it.

**BDNF**

Brain Derived Neurotropic Factor (BDNF) is another substance that has been found in the brain. One of its primary roles seems to be to promote the health, growth and adaptability of nerve cells. It has also been shown to protect the brain from the damaging effects of excess glutamate.

Studies show that individuals with lower amounts of BDNF had higher rates of depression. Likewise, those being treated with anti-depressants did not respond as well to therapy if their level of BDNF was in the lowest percentile.

While these studies did not refer specifically to anxiety per se, they *did* point to the important role of this substance in keeping the brain healthy and in balance (which, as we know by now, is critical to reducing the anxiety response). BDNF also seems to play an important role in enhancing memory formation.

Other substances are currently being studied for their role in emotional and psychological well-being, and are found in some highly unlikely places. Oxytocin, a substance secreted by the posterior pituitary gland in the brain, which is usually associated with contraction of the uterus during childbirth and letdown of milk in the breasts during breast feeding, has also been shown to lessen anxiety and foster positive social interactions. Could that be an intended side effect for soothing both new mothers and their infants? Oxytocin is even being looked at for its possible beneficial role in social phobias.

Scientists have further demonstrated that oxytocin can decrease the production of the CEO stress hormone (corticotropin releasing hormone) in the brain. This action seems to occur because oxytocin has access to the same receptors that the calming neurotransmitter GABA uses. This ultimately leads to reduced stress or anxiety response by the adrenal glands.

To further expand on the benefits of oxytocin, a study published in *Journal of Psychoneuroendocrinology* showed that increased levels of oxytocin induced by positive bonding experiences promoted faster wound healing. Simply stated, having a relationship that makes you feel good not only changes your brain chemistry, it also helps your body to heal faster. In other words, your emotional and psychological well-being is always connected to and affects your physical well-being.

Patients often feel that there is a "pill for every ill," and sometimes pharmaceuticals are part of the answer for varying degrees of the anxiety response. However, we cannot underestimate the role

of nutrition, environment and social interaction on general mental and

psychological well-being.

We've already seen the power of amino acids, which come

from a healthy, balanced diet, and now we see the impact that a

soothing, healthy relationship can have on relieving stress. Remember

the holistic approach to wellness is about creating a harmonious

relationship with all aspects of your life.

## The Anxiety Response and Neurotransmitters:
### *A Simplified Summary*

| Neurotransmitter | Derived from | Actions | Can be affected by |
|---|---|---|---|
| **Serotonin** | L-Tryptophan | Calming, creates a sense of satisfaction<br><br>Too little can contribute to anxiety | High stress levels<br>Inflammation<br>Diet |
| **Glutamate** | L-Glutamine | Excitatory<br><br>Helps with memory | Low Vitamin B6 can increase levels |

| | | Excess can fuel anxiety | |
| --- | --- | --- | --- |
| | | Excess can be toxic to cells | |
| **GABA** | L-Glutamine | Calming | Low Vitamin B6 can decrease levels |
| | | | Poor diet |
| | | | High stress levels |
| **Norepinephrine** | L-Tyrosine | Excitatory | Poor diet |
| | | Improves ability to focus | Brain trauma |
| | | Excess can cause anxiety | |
| **BDNF** | | Nourishes nerve cells and helps them to grow and adapt | Lack of nurturing relationships |
| | | Enhances moods | Lack of exercise |
| | | Improves memory | Negative thinking |
| | | | Vitamin D levels |

## Electricity and the Brain

We have seen the important role that neurotransmitters play in the brain while acting as chemical messengers between the neurons. But another important way that neurons communicate with each other is via electrical changes referred to as "brainwaves" when measured with an EEG (electroencephalogram).

This type of brain communication was discovered by researchers in the 1930s and 1940s. Traditionally, four types of brainwave patterns have been identified (designated by letters of the Greek alphabet):

1. **Beta**

2. **Alpha**

3. **Theta**

4. **Delta**

These brainwaves are measured in cycles per second, or hertz. The higher frequency brainwaves are associated with being more alert. **Beta** brainwaves are between 13 and 38 hertz and are high when we are conscious, actively thinking and alert. Excess beta waves can trigger feelings of fear and anxiety.

**Alpha** brainwaves (8-13 hz) are the next frequency down. They are high when we are physically and mentally relaxed, but still very aware. This is often referred to as focused relaxation, and learning is thought to be enhanced during this time. **Theta** waves (4-7 hz) are associated with being sleepy or deep relaxation. **Delta**, the slowest wave (4 hz), is associated with deep sleep or unconsciousness.

Since the discovery of the above four traditional brainwave patterns, others have been identified and, one in particular, the SMR (sensory motor rhythm) is about 14 hertz and has been looked at in several neurofeedback studies to increase focus and efficiency. This wave form seems to have the ability to link the brain and the body. It was first discovered in cats, where it was noted to prevent seizures.

Even though I have mentioned brainwave patterns as if they occur in isolation, they do not. Overall brain activity comprises all of the brainwave patterns simultaneously. It is our activity levels that help to determine which one is dominant. Ideally, a healthy brain is flexible enough to shift patterns quickly, depending on activity levels, and resilient enough to rebound from environment, such as smoking or medications, poor lifestyle patterns such as lack of sleep, and emotional and physical trauma.

What, then, is neurofeedback? Neurofeedback is a form of therapy that helps to train the brain to increase resilience and flexibility by enhancing its ability to self-regulate. For example, it would be like a dancer trying to learn a complicated series of movements. He may have watched the instructors several times, but just can't seem to position his body correctly when asked to do the routine on his own. It is only when he sees himself reflected in a mirror that he is able to really connect what the proper positioning feels like or, in clinical terms, to "self-regulate."

Another example is when you are learning to ride a bike for the first time. The brain is receiving constant feedback from the body and your muscles: "Oh, you are leaning too much to the right, now the left, now back to the right again."

With this constant feedback, the brain self-regulates, forms a new neural pathway and, bingo, you can ride a bike! Now, you may need assistance such as training wheels (EEG feedback) until you form that pathway; but, once it is established, you never forget. You may get rusty and be a bit wobbly if you haven't ridden in a while, but you never forget.

In this non-invasive form of therapy, sensors are attached to the scalp to record and visualize an individual brainwave pattern. This way, the brain is able to see what patterns need regulation and adjust accordingly. In some instances, the brainwaves are presented on the screen as actual wave patterns and you learn to regulate through manipulation of these patterns.

In other forms of neurofeedback, the brain is presented with information about how it's working through a running visual such as a movie or an ongoing audio, such as a song. When the brainwave patterns become unstable, then the movie or song is briefly interrupted (i.e., the movie briefly dims or the song briefly fades out) and the brain recognizes the disruption and regulates to bring the event back online. As this continues to happen, the brain then creates a pathway to minimize disruption and maximize performance.

Does it work for anxiety? Several studies suggest that neurofeedback would be a helpful adjunct in the treatment of anxiety. One study looked at patients two to three days after they had suffered a cardiac event. Those who received feedback therapy every two weeks for five sessions showed significantly less anxiety than those who received no treatment.

Another study looked at increasing skill level and decreasing anxiety in a group of ophthalmic (eye) microsurgeons using self-regulatory neurofeedback. They were divided into three groups. Two groups had eight 30-minute sessions of EEG training (neurofeedback), and the last group did not have any treatment.

Of the two groups that received feedback sessions, one worked on increasing their SMR waves while decreasing theta waves, while the other group worked on increasing alpha waves while decreasing theta waves. Both groups receiving feedback therapy improved in skill level and reduced anxiety.

The SMR (sensory motor rhythm) group did better than the alpha group. However, there was no improvement in the group that did not receive EEG training. As one can imagine, feeling more focused and skilled in one's daily life can go a long way to reducing anxiety levels.

**Case Study:** *Mary*

Probing deeper for the source of her continuing anxiety, I eventually tested levels of Mary's neurotransmitters. Not surprisingly, we were both "anxious" to get her results. Ultimately, the tests revealed elevated levels of norepinephrine, epinephrine and glutamate.

Her GABA levels were within the normal range; but, given the excess of the excitatory neurotransmitters (norepinephrine, epinephrine and glutamate) in her system, this level was insufficient to balance the anxiety-provoking effects of the excitatory ones. Her serotonin levels were also extremely low.

While Mary was relieved to hear that there was, in fact, a biological "root cause" for her anxiety-producing symptoms, the fact remained that we still had to come up with a plan to resolve her issues. Still, it was a beginning and Mary was eager to get started on her road to recovery.

**Case Study:** *Jennifer*

I also tested Jennifer's neurotransmitter levels in an effort to isolate the potential cause of her continuing anxiety as well. Jennifer's serotonin level was low, but not as low as Mary's. The rest of her neurotransmitter levels were within normal limits.

It would seem that some of Jennifer's anxiety symptoms were due to her low serotonin level. Studies show that serotonin levels start decreasing as we approach the age of 30 and tend to be on a steady decline thereafter, which could account for a noticeable dip in Jennifer's levels and an accommodating rise in anxiety.

**Case Study:** *Josh*

Finally, after running the same set of tests on Josh, I was surprised to find that his serotonin levels were some of the lowest I have ever seen in decades of clinical experience. The rest of his neurotransmitters were within the normal range except for his dopamine, which was slightly low.

# Chapter 4:

## *The Immune System's Connection to Anxiety*

"What in the world does the immune system have to do with anxiety?" you may be asking yourself as you read the title for this chapter. As it turns out, quite a lot! Don't believe me? Try this simple experiment: Let your mind drift back to an illness you may have experienced in your life, maybe even recently. It could have been the flu, a nasty sinus infection or even a common cold.

Didn't you feel depressed, moody or even anxious? Were you not just physically miserable, but emotionally unhappy as well? Wasn't there a moment there, just as your fever broke, your sinuses or your nausea cleared up where, absent your "sick" symptoms, your spirit soared to think that you were finally "getting better"?

Are those feelings totally unrelated to the symptoms? Hardly! That was your immune system actually – and actively – communicating with your nervous system, creating an alert to let you know that something is amiss in both your body *and* your mind.

One extreme example of an infection creating a significant psychological change in the brain is a syndrome known as Pediatric Autoimmune Neuropsychiatric Disorder Associated with Streptococcus, or PANDAS for short.

Children afflicted with this syndrome can develop a severe case of obsessive compulsive disorder following an infection with the streptococcus bacteria. While such cases aren't common, it just goes to show how strongly the body and the mind are connected.

So why should anxiety be any different?


**Inflammation and Anxiety:** *The Critical Link*

The dysfunction of the immune system that leads to chronic inflammation seems to play a role in the development of other diseases as well. For example, more and more research is pointing toward inflammation as a significant causative factor in the development of cardiovascular disease and strokes.

The role of inflammation is considered so important in the development of future diseases that the measurement of a specific marker of inflammation called cardiac c-reactive protein (CRP) is fast

becoming a standard test, in additional to cholesterol, to assess the

risk for development of heart disease and strokes.

Rheumatoid arthritis, an autoimmune disease, is also

associated with a significant increase in inflammation, especially of

pro-inflammatory markers called "cytokines."

For some reason not yet known, these cytokines also seem to

play an important role in the development of psychiatric disorders

such as anxiety and depression. This could be one of the reasons why

individuals with autoimmune diseases, and even heart disease,

develop a higher rate of mood disorders.

Rheumatoid arthritis and other autoimmune diseases are often

treated with medications designed to suppress these cytokines. Do we

then treat anxiety with immunosuppressants, or is the cost too high? It

is only by understanding the basics of how and to what degree the

immune system contributes to anxiety that we can hope to answer that

question and find that all-important balance between the symptoms

and the cure that the body and mind both need to stay healthy.

A compilation of recent research supports the immune system's connection to psychological disorders and, in particular, anxiety. This was illustrated in a variety of recent studies. In one such study, researchers orally administered bacteria to mice and noticed that, shortly thereafter, the mice started exhibiting significant symptoms of anxiety. Interestingly, these mice did not otherwise appear to be sick and it was noted that the anxiety symptoms appeared well before the infection could have entered the blood circulation.

These findings seem to suggest a kind of internal "early alert system" that uses the direct connection of the vagus and other nerves to the brain to signal the anxiety response in the presence of certain stimuli – kind of like an air raid siren can be used to warn small towns of approaching tornadoes.

Studies suggest that the bacteria themselves may be able to use the vagus nerve as a transportation system, either by directly attaching to it, or indirectly by sending its workers, toxins and cytokines, along for the ride instead. This direct communication with the brain puts the nervous system on high alert and, therefore, the body on high alert as well.

## The Enemy Within

Remember, the stress and fear (fight or flight) system was designed as an "alert" of sorts, a prehistoric warning system to protect animals (like us!) from harm or encroaching danger. Initially, it was thought that the stimulus from anxiety always came from an external source, such as a violent predator crouching in the bushes, an emotional stressor like starting a new job or moving to a new town, or some other adverse external event or potential danger like two cars getting into an accident in front of you.

However, imagine if the stimulus causing the constant feeling of anxiety that drove you to pick up this book was actually coming from within and, therefore, was constantly with you causing your system to remain on high alert. What if it wasn't external, after all? What if it was internal, like a stranger prank calling you from your very own attic, and you *couldn't* escape? You, too, might start acting like these mice from the experiment, where normal everyday activity generates such anxiety and fear that you are exhausted by the end of the day, without having faced any actual, real danger!

In other animal studies relevant to our understanding of the anxiety response, scientists used small parasites to trigger inflammation in the colon. This inflammation in the colon is commonly referred to as "colitis." The study used parasites that were not capable of crossing the intestinal wall and entering into circulation. In other words, they only caused inflammation in the lumen (the space in the middle) of the gut.

The researchers found that this inflammation in the colon increased those inflammatory chemicals called "cytokines." These substances were able to cross into the brain and stimulate neurons in the anxiety centers located there to produce anxiety symptoms and behavior. Cytokines can also activate the hypothalamic pituitary adrenal axis and, if we recall, this system governs the body's "fight or flight" response through production of stress hormones by the adrenal glands.

Once this system gets going, it can be self-perpetuating, initiating a chain reaction of hormones that produce anxiety symptoms that produce more hormones that produce more anxiety symptoms, and so on and so forth. For example, activation of the HPA axis causes the release of corticotropin releasing hormone (CRH), the master stress hormone in the brain.

This hormone then acts on the neurons to make them more responsive to the actions of the inflammatory cytokines, thereby facilitating the anxiety response. When individuals were given a substance that decreased the effect that the hormone CRH had on the neurons, then these specialized nerve cells did not respond as strongly to the inflammatory cytokines and the participants in the study showed decreased levels of anxiety symptoms and behavior.

Interestingly, these inflammatory cytokines are produced not only by the immune cells but can also be produced in other cells of the body, such as fat cells and the glial cells that surround the nerve cells in the brain. To clarify, there are many different types of cytokines; some produce inflammation and are referred to as "pro-inflammatory," and others are actually considered "anti-inflammatory."

You may be familiar with some of these terms from over-the-counter medicine ads, but this section will help define them and how they may relate to your recurring anxiety symptoms.

Some of the inflammatory cytokines identified in the anxiety response are interleukin-1 (IL-1), tumor necrosis factor alpha (TNF-a) and interleukin-6 (IL-6). Interestingly, these are some of the same cytokines identified in rheumatoid arthritis.

How are these substances able to affect so many systems at once? It turns out that there are receptors for these inflammatory cytokines present on immune cells, nerve cells *and* cells in the endocrine system. Therefore, cytokines are able to bind to these cells and, essentially, "turn them on."

There are several other ways that the immune system seems to play a role in activating the anxiety response. I described earlier how the amino acid tryptophan, which makes serotonin, is metabolized via two primary pathways. The first pathway produces serotonin, which is responsible for relaxation, and melatonin, which helps us sleep.

The second pathway can produce substances that can be potentially irritating to the brain and its neurons. Cytokines in particular, which as we know are created by infection and inflammation, can accelerate the formation of these "brain irritants" by speeding up the enzyme that pushes the second reaction forward. In fact, several cytokines, including IL-1, TNF-alpha and interferon gamma, have all been implicated in this process. Interestingly, cortisol, the stress hormone made by the adrenal glands, is also capable of increasing the rate of this reaction. In the figure on the next page, we can see that once this reaction gets going it can become self-perpetuating, or create its own fuel.

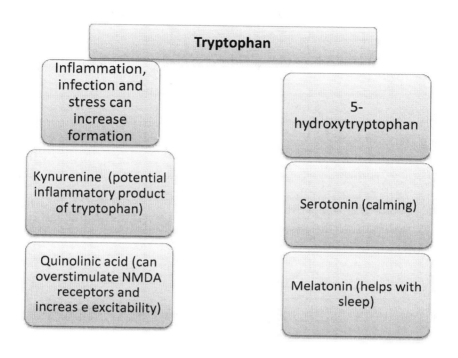

**Figure 4.1:** *How anxiety creates its own "fuel."*

Now, here's a review of the steps involved in this reaction to see how they all work together to make you more anxious:

1. **Ready, Set, Stress!** In the first step, the stress response gets activated – whether by an external stressor such as a sudden scare, or an emotional event, or by infection in the gut.

2. **HPA Away!** The stressor (or the inflammatory cytokines produced by an infection) acts on the neurons in the amygdala, ultimately stimulating the HPA axis.

3. **The Cortisol (and Adrenaline) Connection.** This ultimately sends messages through the body to the adrenal glands to produce cortisol and adrenaline.

4. **A Byproduct of Tryptophan.** Excess cortisol can then affect the way the body metabolizes tryptophan, thereby creating an inflammatory substance called quinolinic acid.

5. **Stimulation, Plus.** This can then go on to overstimulate NMDA receptors and potentially exacerbate the stress and anxiety response.

6. **Memory Matters.** Additionally, cortisol can have a direct impact on cells in the memory part of the brain called the "hippocampus," ultimately creating issues with short-term memory. Many individuals who experience anxiety symptoms for an extended period of time can start exhibiting issues with accessing short term memory.

## Why Do We Grow More Anxious With Age?

As if all that weren't enough, it turns out that aging seems to be independently associated with an increase in these inflammatory cytokines, such as interferon gamma and tumor necrosis alpha. One of the effects of chronic exposure to these cytokines seems to be the loss of sensitivity to the feedback mechanism – or safety valve "shut off" system – that is set up between the brain and the body.

For example, when the pituitary gland requests cortisol from the adrenal glands to support a stress response and cortisol eventually reaches a certain level, it signals the brain that "enough is enough." In turn, the brain then "turns off" the demand for more cortisol, thereby allowing levels to go back to normal. It's the same way your toilet tank knows to turn off the water after you flush; a little ball, or sensor, "senses" the water level is full and stops running.

As we get older and those cytokines increase, this feedback system begins to fail so that the brain never gets the message to stop the waterworks. As a result, the master hormone in the brain that stimulates the formation of cortisol in the body doesn't shut off. This chemical oversight allows circulating cortisol levels to remain high, thus directly and indirectly affecting the immune system and various nerve cells.

Imagine having no chemical valve in place to essentially "shut off" the hormones that produce symptoms of anxiety. It is believed that this is one of the reasons that the elderly are more prone to symptoms of anxiety and depression than the rest of the population.

Research into the medications frequently used to combat depression and anxiety further supports the important role that the immune system plays in our emotional and physical well-being.

So, how do the prescriptions we take to ease our anxieties actually work? Studies show that medications targeted at specific neurotransmitters such as selective serotonin reuptake inhibitors (SSRI) and tricyclic anti-depressants (TCA) not only increase the amount of the targeted neurotransmitters available for use in the brain, but they also decrease the levels of inflammatory cytokines, thus decreasing inflammation.

How does it work? Most anti-depressant medications achieve maximum results in 6-8 weeks and it seems that this is about the same time frame that it takes to significantly affect the levels of circulating cytokines. Several studies show that the levels of neurotransmitters themselves are actually increased much earlier, but the full clinical effect of the medication seems to coincide with the lowering of the cytokine levels.

It seems the old adage "you are what you think" may also affect our immune system and our emotional state. Research supports the fact that not only do increased pro-inflammatory cytokines such as TNF-alpha contribute toward anxiety and negative thinking, but negative thinking increases inflammatory cytokines as well.

Again, once the old self-perpetuating "anxiety wheel" starts spinning, it seems to be capable of generating just enough wind to keep it going. I am sure at this point you are starting to see that managing this deceptively simple condition is going to require a multi-pronged approach, which is why it's so critical that you and your treating physician work together to arrive at a suitable treatment plan. Arming yourself with the basic, physiological facts about how the anxiety response works is one critical step in the right direction.

## The Story of Inflammation:

| Increased by | Lab Test to Identify | Can Cause |
|---|---|---|
| Infection | hs-CRP | Increased stress hormones |
| Obesity | Omega-s/Arachidonic acid ratio | Increased anxiety |
| Poor nutrition | Cytokine levels (more complicated) | Decreased formation of serotonin |
| Increased age | | Increased negative thinking |
| Negative thinking | | |

Figure 4.2: *Inflammation in a nutshell*

**Case Studies:** *Mary and Jennifer*

In a continued effort to determine the levels of various hormones in both Mary and Jennifer, I ran a few additional tests on both women. The inflammatory marker cardiac CRP, or C-reactive protein, was normal for both women. (As you'll recall, CRP is fast becoming a standard test, in addition to cholesterol, to assess risk for development of heart disease and strokes.)

CRP may also be an indication that pro-inflammatory cytokines are elevated, thus helping to determine if inflammation could be part of what is fueling the anxiety symptoms.

**Case Study:** *Josh*

When given the same CRP test, Josh had a mild elevation in his C-reactive protein level, suggesting that inflammation might be contributing not only to his anxiety and insomnia, but also to his high blood pressure.

Stress wasn't the only issue on the table as a result of Josh's test readings. I was also concerned that this increase in inflammation, coupled with his high cholesterol, could also increase his risk for

vascular disease.

# Chapter 5:

## *Your Gut and the Anxiety Connection*

I previously alluded to the gut's role when it comes to provoking anxiety in the chapter on the immune system. Here, I will attempt to develop this intricate process a bit further.

Let's start with one reason why you really do "feel" emotions in your gut. That could be because the gut has more than 100 million neurons. Yes, neurons! This means that the gut has a nervous system all of its own. This is referred to as the "visceral," or "enteric," nervous system and 90 percent of the neurons have a connection to the brain.

Remember that neurotransmitter serotonin and the powerful role it plays in the anxiety response? Well, 90 percent of the serotonin in the body is found in the gut! The role of serotonin in the gut is not yet fully understood; however, it is thought to play a role in gastrointestinal motility.

One theory for why serotonin is so prevalent in the gut is that it may be part of a defensive mechanism designed to keep your body free of harmful toxins, as we'll soon see. Most of the serotonin found in the gut is bound and, therefore, inactive. When the gut is exposed to certain toxins, it can stimulate the release of large amounts of serotonin, causing (sorry in advance)… explosive diarrhea. While this may sound like an unhealthy condition, the fact is that this volatile act helps to expel harmful toxins with immediacy.

If enough of these toxins aren't expelled via diarrhea, excess serotonin can then stimulate a specific serotonin receptor (5HT3) in the brain, leading to nausea and vomiting to further augment the elimination process. Also, the gut and the immune system have strong ties as the gut contains about 70 percent of the body's immunity.

Recent work within the scientific community on the gut's role in emotional health is beginning to shed light on this interactive process. A big "aha" moment in the body-slash-mind connection came recently when researchers were able to prove that the amount and the type of bacteria in the gut (body) have a direct impact on our behavior (mind).

Most of us are aware of probiotics (good bacteria) and their role in maintaining a healthy immune system, improving symptoms of constipation and helping us to ward off diarrhea and yeast infections after antibiotic usage. After all, everything from TV yogurt commercials to magazine articles and blog posts lately have touted the healthy nature of probiotics and their role in alleviating the above conditions, but… changing our behavior? Well, that is big news to most of us.

Yet in one experiment, science has shown an incredible link in the role of probiotics and emotional health. In the study, researchers used three strains of mice:

1.) Mice bred for their passive and reserved personality traits;

2.) Mice bred for their active, outgoing personalities; and

3.) Germ-free mice (i.e., mice without bacteria in the intestine).

The scientists then colonized the germ-free mice with the bacteria from the active, "outgoing" mice and, amazingly, the first group exhibited the same outgoing social behavior of the more socially active mice. Then they colonized germ-free mice with bacteria from passive mice, and their behavior reflected that of passive mice.

Several other studies supported this finding linking the intriguing bacteria-behavior connection. One study treated anxious mice with a course of antibiotics and found that many of the anxiety symptoms disappeared, only to return when the antibiotics were stopped. This suggested that there might be a particular strain of bacteria that may have triggered anxiety symptoms.

The results looked clear cut, so the quest was on to figure out if this response was bacteria specific or if it was dependent on the production of other substances. While the question may be far from being answered in its entirety, several interesting observations have been made along the way.

Apparently, given recent evidence, several factors seem to be at work in this chain of events. Studies using the probiotic Lactobacilli rhamnosus administered orally showed that it enhanced the function of the calming, or inhibitory, neurotransmitter GABA. The levels of the corresponding stress hormone in mice, corticosterone, were also reduced.

This resulted in the reversal of the anxiety symptoms in the mice being studied. This effect seemed to be mediated by the vagus nerve, as the benefits of administering this probiotic were lost when the vagus nerve was cut so that it no longer communicated with the brain. It was noted in the immune chapter that infections such as infectious colitis induced an anxiety response in animals studied. When the probiotic Bifidobacterium longum NCC3001 was administered to the mice with infectious colitis, it again reduced the symptoms of anxiety.

Once again, it was noted that this effect did not occur if the vagus nerve was cut so that there was no communication with the brain. Interestingly, this probiotic seemed to have no effect on the inflammatory cytokines produced by the infection. Remember that inflammatory cytokines can stimulate the anxiety response. So, in essence, this experiment proved the probiotic's effect on anxiety did not depend on its ability to affect inflammatory cytokines.

Then what, you might ask, could be other potential mechanisms of action? It seems that Bifidobacterium longum increased the production of brain derived neurotropic factor (BDNF), thus increasing protection to the neurons against the excitatory neurotransmitter glutamate.

To truly see if decreasing inflammatory cytokines would have an effect on anxiety, the immune suppressant Enbrel (normally used to treat autoimmune diseases like rheumatoid arthritis) was administered to test mice and, lo and behold, the symptoms of anxiety *did* abate. (There was also no corresponding increase in BDNF.)

Mind you, this is not to suggest that we should suppress the immune system in order to treat anxiety, which would actually lead to a host of other presenting problems, but rather to illustrate the intricacies of the process involved in the research so that we can appreciate the complexities of symptom management.

## What You Experience Could Affect How You Feel

We've talked a lot about internal factors and how they make you feel, but now let's turn our attention to the external, "out of body" factors that might cause, or even alleviate, stress. One interesting point to note is that researchers have also discovered that environmental and psychological stressors can actually change the makeup of the bacterial flora in the gut.

Specifically, it was shown that stress can encourage the growth of one species of bacteria while inhibiting the growth of another. For example, one study showed that being stressed can actually increase the growth of the bacteria species Clostridium and, as a result, this can create pathology (i.e., do harm) in the human gut.

It was also demonstrated that stress itself can increase the production of the inflammatory cytokines such as interleukin-6 (IL-6), thus further perpetuating the anxiety response. Let's just appreciate for a moment that all this redundancy and intricacy was set up by the body to ensure our safety in a time when any decrease in alertness could be fatal.

Today, however, it is the constant activation of this system that is harming us. Very few of us face danger on a daily basis, and yet so many of us are anxious far too often for our own good. The density of this chapter was necessary to help us all understand how closely our bodies are aligned with our brains, and how even something like the stomach can play such a large role in the anxiety response.

Let's revisit bacteria for a moment before we move on. Another function of having the right type and amount of "good bacteria" in the gut is helping with the production and absorption of vitamins such as biotin, folic acid and vitamin K. Low folic acid levels have been associated with low serotonin levels and, in many studies, folic acid has been shown to augment the effectiveness of anti-depressants.

This is important when it comes to treating anxiety because oftentimes anti-depressants are used to treat stress-related symptoms – upset stomach, butterflies, indigestion, etc. – and many times depression accompanies anxiety, especially in women.

## Can What You Eat Make You More Anxious?

Brace yourself: This section is going to delve into the role of food sensitivities in perpetuating the anxiety response. Case in point: Studies show that chronic stress can increase the permeability of the lining of the intestinal wall. What the heck does *that* mean? Well, if this occurs, then particles that were once too large to cross the barrier and enter into the circulation are now able to do so more easily, causing untold harm outside the digestive system.

For example, if partially digested food crosses into the circulation before it has been broken down to its smallest particles, this can stimulate the immune system to act as though this food is now a foreign substance (antigen) invading the body. Certain bacteria, such as H. Pylori, can also affect the permeability of the gastric (stomach) mucosa and thus increase the risk of developing food sensitivities or immune response to certain foods.

Since, as we've learned, a full 70 percent of the body's immune system is in the gut, sensitivity to foods and the subsequent inflammation that it produces could potentially intensify the anxiety response and disrupt bacterial flora, further exacerbating symptoms.

Here again it seems that there is another probiotic to the rescue. Bifidobacterium Animalis Lactis LKM 512 has been shown in studies to tighten the junction of the gut lining, thus decreasing permeability, decreasing inflammation in the elderly and suppressing inflammatory bacteria.

Another issue that can be related to dysfunction in the gut is the ability of the gastrointestinal system to appropriately digest and absorb foods to maximize the extraction of much-needed nutrients. Several factors can affect the digestive process. First, digestive enzymes need to be present in the appropriate amount. A decrease in the digestive enzyme in the stomach, pancreas and small intestines and bile from the gall bladder can negatively impact the gastrointestinal system's ability to prepare foods for absorption.

If Betaine HCL and pepsin levels are too low in the stomach, then the initial digestion and preparation of protein for further digestion is decreased. If the stomach is not functioning optimally, then absorption of important vitamins and minerals such as vitamin B12 and zinc can be affected as well. As we get older, we trend toward producing less and less stomach acid. Also, certain conditions such as atrophic gastritis and pernicious anemia can affect our ability to absorb vitamin B12.

If pancreatic enzymes, i.e., the enzymes present on the walls of the small intestines, are insufficient, then digestion of proteins, fats and carbohydrates can be adversely affected. As we have already noted, it is important that proteins are broken down to their smallest components, namely amino acids.

These amino acids are necessary for the production of key neurotransmitters in the stress response. Bile plays a key role in the digestion and preparation of fats for absorption. In studies, key fats such as omega-3 polyunsaturated fatty acids and the fat-soluble vitamin D have been shown to support brain health and play a part in management of anxiety and other psychological disorders.

## Case Study: *Mary*

Mary's reports of significant gastrointestinal symptoms naturally concerned me, and prompted us to perform a comprehensive stool analysis early on in her medical evaluation. We needed to get an idea if the bacterial flora in the gut was balanced. We also needed to answer some critical questions, such as:

- **Were there any pathological bacteria, such as H. Pylori, present in her gut?**

- **Were there any parasites?**

- **Did it look like she had sufficient "good" bacteria?**

Other issues evaluated were markers of insufficient digestion and absorption that might be present. For example, did it look like Mary was absorbing fats well? Her results revealed the presence of H. Pylori, insufficient friendly bacteria and evidence of inefficient protein absorption, any of which – let alone in combination – could be contributing to her anxiety symptoms.

# Chapter 6:

## *The Link Between Anxiety and Hormones*

Not only can anxiety symptoms be linked directly to issues with the gut, but they can also be perpetuated by an imbalance of several hormones in the body. It has been noted that women suffer from anxiety at rates four times that of their male counterparts, yet it is only recently that studies are being focused on identifying the potential cause of this troubling phenomenon.

A recent study conducted by the neuroscientists at Harvard and Emory universities, for instance, revealed that women responded better to stress when their estrogen levels were higher. The study was conducted using the Pavlovian method pairing a noxious stimulus (such as an electrical shock) with a neutral stimulus (such as a color). After a conditioning period where the stimuli were paired, the subjects were shown just the neutral stimulus and then their responses were measured. The findings indicated that the women in the higher estrogen percentile had a much milder response to the neutral stimulus.

To translate this research into everyday language, the women were less on edge and, thus, less likely to respond excessively to non-threatening events. In other words, they were not always waiting for the "other shoe to drop," and therefore every event did not represent the end of the world.

The women with higher estrogen levels, or those who were in various phases of their menstrual cycle (when estrogen levels were typically higher), also responded better to therapy to neutralize fear (otherwise known as "fear extinction").

To further support this hypothesis, women who took the so-called "morning after" pill (which contains both estrogen and progestin) after a traumatic event showed fewer signs of post-traumatic stress disorder than those who did not. One possible reason for these results is that estrogen seems to increase the production of the enzyme tryptophan hydroxylase, which is responsible for the conversion of the amino acid tryptophan to the calming

neurotransmitter serotonin.

Again, isn't it amazing how the various bodily systems are

designed to work in synergy with one another to produce a collective

result? So even in a time of more stress, the presence – and chain

reaction – of one or more hormones working together can reduce

stress.

**Anxiety and Menopause:** *Relief from Suffering*

Other studies seem to support this finding as well. The KEEPS

Study (Kronos Early Estrogens Prevention Study) looked at 727

healthy younger women (with an age range of between 42 and 52

years old) all within one to three years of menopause over the course

of four years. This study was performed as a double blind placebo

study, which is widely recognized as "the gold standard" for scientific

studies.

This is in comparison to the World Health Initiative Study

(WHI), where the average age of the participants was 62 and many

already had significant medical issues such as high blood pressure, high cholesterol, etc. In the KEEPS Study, the women were given low doses of estrogen and progesterone. They were divided into three distinct groups:

1. **Low-dose estrogen as patch with progesterone such as prometrium**
2. **Low-dose oral estrogen (premarin) with progesterone**
3. **Placebo**

The summary of results clearly revealed that those taking low-dose oral estrogen reported more relief from anxiety-type symptoms that often accompany menopause than those using the patch, and the oral dose was definitely more effective than placebo. Both the patch and oral estrogen users also reported relief from symptoms of menopause, such as hot flashes and insomnia.

So, while those participants who received either the oral or patch doses of estrogen found relief, placebo users did not, leading to a clear link between estrogen – both in oral and patch form – and reduced suffering from anxiety and other issues associated with menopause.

There were some other interesting findings from this particular study as well. Case in point: Oral doses of estrogen were found to increase HDL (otherwise known as "good" cholesterol), LDL (i.e., "bad" cholesterol) and triglycerides. The patch estrogen improved insulin resistance, which means better blood sugar management, but did not affect cholesterol or triglycerides levels. Also, there did not appear to be any significant increase in blood pressure, blood clots, uterine or breast cancer discovered in either of the two groups that received estrogen in either form.

What's unique about this study is that it is still ongoing, so hopefully it can also answer the question: "How long is it safe to use hormonal therapy?" As many of you know, hormone therapy is a very topical subject these days and many of us are curious not only about the safety of the therapy itself, but the longevity of using hormone therapy. Studies such as this one can go a long way toward alleviating our fears, or even confirming them.

The "take home" points from this particular study, which was presented at the North American Menopause Society's annual meeting in Orlando in 2012, include the fact that healthy women seem to do well during the early phases of menopause. If you are at risk for diabetes and lipid issues, however, then work with your doctor to determine if and in what form hormone replace therapy, or HRT, might be right for you.

## The Link Between Testosterone and Other Reproductive Hormones and Anxiety

Studies are also pointing to the important role of testosterone in controlling anxiety symptoms, and not just in men. "The Netherlands Study of Depression and Anxiety," published in the *Journal of Psychosomatic Research 2012,* looked at salivary testosterone levels in 720 males and 1,380 females. They found that women diagnosed with generalized anxiety disorder, social phobias and depression had lower testosterone levels.

In women suffering from polycystic ovarian syndrome, a condition marked by elevated testosterone and insulin levels, studies show a greater occurrence of anxiety and depressive symptoms when compared to women who did not have the disorder (and thus had lower levels of testosterone in their systems). These findings once again underscore the need for hormonal balance in order to optimize function.

I always recommend that, if you're having trouble properly diagnosing, or even treating, your anxiety symptoms that you urge your treating physician(s) to search high and low for the cause, particularly in light of what research tells us about how these hormones interact with each other and reflect back in the form of anxiety – or even treating anxiety.

Several other studies have made a distinct connection between low testosterone and depression in men. To understand their relevance, let's consider the production of, and uses for, testosterone in the body. A quick primer: Testosterone is produced in the testicles and adrenal glands in males and in the ovaries and adrenal glands in females. In males, testosterone levels peak at about age 22 and start declining one percent a decade after about age 35. Several studies have pointed toward testosterone's role in protecting the brain cells in males, as well as preventing a sharp cognitive decline.

The role of the other reproductive hormones such as progesterone may play a role in the anxiety response as well. Progesterone is the hormone that works in concert with estrogen to regulate the menstrual cycle and prepare the body for pregnancy. It is produced primarily in the ovaries. In some studies, progesterone has been shown to have an anxiolytic effect. (In other words, it reduces anxiety.)

In animal studies, progesterone has demonstrated the ability to help form the protective sheath of fat that covers the neurons, called myelin. This helps the nerve cells to communicate with each other better. Progesterone is also metabolized into allopregnanolone in the body. This metabolite acts on the GABA-A receptors and has an extreme calming effect on the mind, thus potentially modulating anxiety and improving related symptoms such as insomnia. Hormones like this one, which act directly on sites designated for neurotransmitters, are sometimes referred to as "neuro-active steroids."

Pregnenolone, not to be confused with progesterone, is the starting hormone that is then subsequently converted to the other sex hormones (DHEA, progesterone, testosterone and estrogen) and the stress hormone cortisol. Many times one is able to purchase pregnenolone over the counter and it is sold as a substance to support hormones, memory and stress levels. Studies show that this hormone can be potentially anxiogenic or, in other words, cause anxiety.

In low amounts, pregnenolone does work to activate the GABA-A (calming) receptors to help with anxiety, but higher amounts actually block these receptors, which can lead to anxiety. Also, when injected directly into the amygdala (or the "fear center" of the brain), low-dose pregnenolone was shown to enhance memory retention.

Particularly relevant to the anxiety response, the presence of pregnenolone makes it easier to unlearn a fear behavior. Known as "fear extinction," unlearning fear behaviors is the basis for many anxiety treatment regimens. And, as many of us know, fear and anxiety are inextricably linked and lessening our fear is a sure way to begin reducing the amount, level, and even duration of our anxious periods.

Pregnenolone was also noted to activate the NMDA receptors and, if you recall, overexcitation of this receptor could create anxiety. You'll also recall that memory formation and retention also require activation of these receptors. Therefore, just enough of the hormone can help reduce anxiety, while too much can cause it. Balance just seems to be a consistent theme with the body, and will be a recurring one as we begin to discuss treatment options later in this book.

DHEA, or dehydroepiandrosterone, another hormone that is readily available over the counter, can create anxiety as well. This hormone is often promoted as being able to slow, or even stop, the aging process. While DHEA has been shown to have some benefits, inappropriate use can cause unwanted effects such as anxiety and imbalance of the other hormones that may contribute to anxiety. It seems that DHEA sulfate has the ability to block the GABA- A receptors, thus preventing activation and potentially creating anxiety symptoms.

Cortisol, one of the primary stress hormones produced by the body, has also been shown to be elevated in patients suffering from anxiety. A recent study showed that the morning cortisol levels were particularly susceptible to this increase, especially in anxiety patients who also suffered from depression.

As mentioned in a previous chapter, cortisol is made by the adrenal glands under the direction of the pituitary gland in the brain (HPA axis). If we also recall, the GABA neurotransmitter and oxytocin can ultimately affect the production of this hormone by acting on the brain to reduce the levels of the master stress hormone in the brain (CRH).

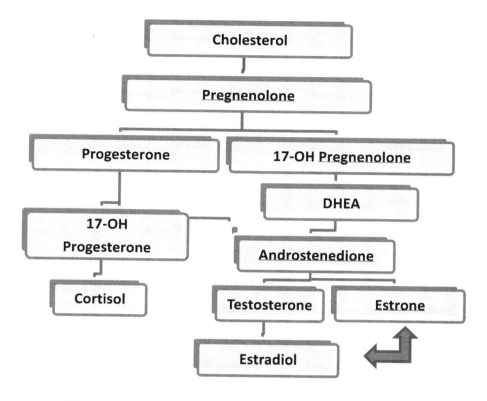

**Figure 6.1:** *Hormones involved in the anxiety response.*

Another hormone associated with anxiety symptoms is the thyroid hormone. While studies are suggesting more depressive-type symptoms with hypo (too little) or hyper (too much) thyroid, anxiety can be a presenting symptom as well.

Interestingly, a study published in *Endocrine Journal* in 2004 revealed that patients with normal thyroid hormones (T4 and T3), but even slightly abnormal Thyroid Stimulating Hormone (a hormone in the brain that stimulates thyroid gland to make hormones) showed an increase in anxiety symptoms.

Clearly, it is important that your thyroid is in balance, as it is imperative that all of your hormones be in balance as well. A period where hormones can get particularly out of whack is during pregnancy. Specifically, pregnancy can be a risk factor for development of thyroid issues.

So while pregnancy itself and sex hormones can cause mood changes, thyroid function should be evaluated during pregnancy and the immediate post-partum period if there is an onset of anxiety symptoms. Several studies tell us individuals will respond better to treatment if thyroid function is optimized.

Other hormones and issues that may also contribute to additional anxiety symptoms are insulin and hypoglycemia. Hypoglycemia, or low blood sugar, can present as anxiety with shakiness, sweating, palpitations and irritability. If fasting insulin levels are elevated, then this can lead to low blood sugar levels as insulin is responsible for removing glucose (sugar) from the blood.

Sometimes it is necessary to do three-hour glucola testing, checking for both glucose levels as well as insulin levels to determine someone who may be at risk for hypoglycemia. This testing can also help to determine those at risk for developing diabetes, as hypoglycemia can be the first sign of blood sugar dysregulation.

## Are Your Habits Making You Anxious?

Could your habits be making you more anxious than not? They very well could be. That's because other factors that contribute toward anxiety symptoms include poor nutrition, substance abuse and overuse of stimulatory substances such as caffeine.

For example, it was noted in a study published in the *Psychiatric Journal* that women with alcohol abuse issues were two to three times as likely to suffer from anxiety disorders than their counterparts who did not abuse alcohol. While many of us use alcohol to cope with our anxiety, be aware that the so-called "cure" could be contributing to greater stress symptoms instead.

Withdrawal from certain medications such as benzodiazepines and beta blockers can also produce anxiety-type symptoms, so it is suggested that a "step down" approach be used, where you gradually reduce the use of such items, instead of a "cold turkey" attempt, which could make you anxious and vulnerable to seizures. It is imperative that you work with your physician during any changes with these medications.

It's long been noted that coffee and soda can make us feel "jittery" if we've had too much. Therefore, it should come as no surprise that overuse of caffeinated beverages can also lead to symptoms of anxiety as well. When presenting with anxiety symptoms, be sure to provide your treating physician with a thorough history of all potential contributors to your stress symptoms, including and up to your daily habits such as how many cups of coffee you drink and what medications you may be taking. After all, even certain aspirins can contain caffeine.

When it comes to alcohol, several studies have shown a decrease in BDNF in the amygdala (fear center) in the brain in individuals with alcohol dependence. Short-term use of alcohol initially enhances the brain's production of BDNF and, in turn, this increases the production of a protein in the nerve cells in the amygdala called the ARC protein. It appears that this protein promotes the formation of extra tiny "arms" at the end of the neurons called dendrites.

These extra spikes enhance the communication between neurons and this seems to have an anti-anxiety effect. When the production of the protein was artificially inhibited, the extra tiny arms disappeared and anxiety levels increased. The disappearance of the spikes also occurred with alcohol withdrawal, thus increasing anxiety symptoms as well. This might be why alcohol initially seems to lessen anxiety symptoms in some individuals.

Animal studies using rats showed that those with genetically lower levels of BNDF and ARC protein exhibited innate anxiety behavior. Alcohol administered to these rats did increase the ARC protein and improve anxiety symptoms.

These animals also increased their consumption of alcohol. In animals that did not have low levels of these chemicals, alcohol seemed not to have the same effect. We may at last be beginning to scratch the surface of addictive behaviors. Ultimately, we know that excessive alcohol damages the brain and the body. Not a good price to pay for anxiety relief.

| Hormones | Produced by | Beneficial Effects | Potentially Adverse Effects |
|---|---|---|---|
| Estrogen | Ovaries<br>Fat cells<br>Adrenals<br>Brain | -Decrease anxiety/ depression<br>-Increase serotonin levels<br>-Improve memory<br>-Improve insulin resistance | -Increased cholesterol (good and bad)<br>-Potential for increased risk of strokes and clots |
| Testosterone | Testes<br>Ovaries<br>Adrenals | Improves anxiety/depression<br>Improves libido | -Increased anxiety and aggression<br>-High levels linked to insulin resistance in women with PCOS |
| Progesterone | Ovaries<br>Adrenals | -Can decrease anxiety<br>-Helps to form myelin | High levels can worsen insulin resistance |
| Cortisol | Adrenals | - Prepares body to react to perceived danger<br>-Keeps inflammation in check | Excess can<br>-Increase anxiety<br>-raise blood sugar levels<br>-Suppress immune system<br>-Cause weight gain<br>-Decrease muscle mass |
| Thyroxine (thyroid hormone) | Thyroid gland | Balances metabolism | Deficiency<br>-Depression/anxiety<br>-High cholesterol<br>-High blood pressure<br>-Low heart function<br>Excess<br>-Anxiety<br>-Palpitation/irregular heart beat |

| | | | -Weight loss |
|---|---|---|---|
| Insulin | Pancreas | Keeps blood sugar level<br>Helps to build muscle | Excess<br>-Hypoglycemia<br>-Insulin resistance, thus increasing diabetes risk<br>-Increased inflammation<br>-Hormone imbalances |

**Figure 6.2:** *A Simple Guide to Hormones and Anxiety*

**Case Study:** *Mary*

So, how did our three test subjects fare when we tested them for hormone levels and their potential contribution to the anxiety response? Well, Mary had already had her hormones and cortisol levels checked. Digging further, her estrogen and progesterone levels were both within normal limits, but her cortisol levels were elevated through the day.

Excess cortisol was driving her anxiety levels by possibly enhancing adrenaline production, making Mary's brain less sensitive to the effects of calming neurotransmitters, and most likely was contributing to the slight increase detected in her blood sugar levels.

**Case Study:** *Jennifer*

Jennifer's estrogen, progesterone and testosterone levels were also normal, but her cortisol level was noted to be low. Jennifer had probably come to a point where her body could no longer keep up with the high demand for the stress hormone. Her low cortisol level could lead to fatigue or lower energy level, low blood sugar levels and low blood pressure.

Part of the plan to replenish her cortisol level had to include managing her anxiety levels, as this was the major source of her energy drain. The possible hypoglycemia perpetuated by her low cortisol levels could also be contributing to her anxiety symptoms.

**Case Study:** *Josh*

Given his age and activity level, Josh showed a significant decrease in his testosterone levels. We would need to find out why his levels were so low, and what to do about them, so that he could attain the "balance" so critical for relieving his anxiety symptoms. His cortisol levels were normal.

# Chapter 7:

## *What to Do – Brain Remedies*

Since there is no specific test for anxiety, per se, a diagnosis must be made after a thorough history, physical exam and, when indicated, studies and tests to rule out possible underlying disorders that may indicate more serious issues than run-of-the-mill anxiety.

For instance, other diseases that can mimic panic or anxiety disorders include abnormal heart rhythms such as supraventricular tachycardia, mitral valve prolapse, coronary artery disease (i.e., blockages in arteries leading to the heart) and, in rare cases, blood clots to the lungs.

Other conditions that could also share symptoms with anxiety disorders include asthma, pheochromocytoma (a tumor on the adrenal glands causing production of too much adrenaline), hypoparathyroidism (a condition leading to low calcium levels, which can further cause abnormal sensation of skin), hyperthyroidism and hypoglycemia.

Now, keep in mind that anxiety disorders are much more common than many of these conditions and that, by sharing your full history and risk factors with your physician, he/she can help to determine if you are at risk for any of the above. These histories are very important, as you can see, so think carefully about your family, personal and physical history before answering, to give the treating physician as broad a spectrum as you possibly can.

Now, let us start treatment from the point where you have ruled out potentially life-threatening illness and other medical conditions and, based on all the evidence at hand, what you have left is anxiety.

So, what is your next step? Well, your first step would be attempting to identify the trigger for whatever anxiety symptoms you presented to your physician with. Is it a situational trigger, such as an event or underlying and unresolved issue? Is it a specific phobia or fear, or is it generalized (i.e., you feel afraid of "everything")?

Once you've identified, as closely as possible, the trigger of the anxiety, we then want to determine what, if anything, is fueling the anxiety response. Are there things such as foods and inflammation adding fuel to the fire? Are you drinking or smoking more to offset the anxiety, but actually contributing to it? Is insomnia adding to the problem?

Finally, we want to look toward a treatment regimen that would be both safe and successful.

But first things first – let's start with the root cause, which we can often determine through a variety of baseline tests.

## Baseline Tests

While there are no specific laboratory tests to diagnose anxiety, there are some lab tests that may help your physician to identify triggers that may be fueling your anxiety, thus allowing him or her to personalize your treatment to reduce those symptoms, or maybe even the causes.

As we've seen throughout this book, there are numerous physical links between the body and the brain and studying them closely, and specifically, can often lead to clues about various anxiety-producing hormones.

For example, how much is the hypothalamic pituitary axis (HPA) contributing to your symptomatology (i.e., your array of anxiety-related symptoms)? Remember, the HPA axis can be triggered by the immune system as well as by emotional or traumatic events. The HPA axis is also one of the primary ways the brain prepares the body for potential action in times of actual, or just perceived, danger.

Once this "fight or flight" system is activated, as you'll no doubt recall, it sends out large amounts of cortisol and adrenaline, two primary chemicals designed to prepare the body for action. Excess or prolonged exposure to these chemicals can leave us living in an almost continuous state of anxiety and "red alert," as discussed previously.

Now remember, excess stress hormones can leave the brain cells more susceptible to the actions of the other anxiety provocateurs such as pro-inflammatory cytokines, once again perpetuating the anxiety cycle.

To keep the balance in check, then, how do we evaluate stress hormone levels? There are several ways to evaluate the role that cortisol plays in the stress response and, as with most things, each method has certain benefits and limitations.

As a reminder, the level of our stress hormone cortisol has been shown to be highest in the morning before gradually decreasing throughout the day. That probably shouldn't come as a surprise to many of us. Just think of waking up in the morning as perhaps one of the most "stressful" transitions you will making throughout the day.

Ideally, you are going from a peaceful slumber to being alert and ready for your day, all in a matter of moments. The natural progression of cortisol is to slowly decrease throughout the day, falling to its lowest point at night so that we can then fall under the peaceful influence of melatonin (your "sleep hormone") and drift gently off to sleep. If this pattern is disrupted, for example, evidenced by low levels of cortisol in the morning when a high level is needed and high levels at night that keep us awake, one can see the potential for developing insomnia, fatigue and anxiety.

Checking the level of cortisol in the morning, along with the master hormone ACTH, will give us a snapshot of our stress pattern in the morning. It will answer some serious questions as well, such as:

- **Do we have enough stress hormones to keep us awake and alert?**
- **Do we have so much stress hormone that we wake up jittery and anxious?**
- **Or, are our stress hormone levels so low that it takes all of our efforts to put one foot in front of the other?**

Checking these levels early in the morning is convenient and gives us information for that moment in time. But, what about the rest of the day? What are our stress hormone levels doing, say, at lunchtime or late afternoon or even early evening? That is the drawback of this method of early morning-only testing: it gives us one moment in time, and one moment only.

Other methods that seek to overcome this drawback are saliva testing of cortisol levels and measurement of stress hormones in the urine collected over a 24-hour period.

Unlike "morning-only" testing, salivary testing of cortisol levels can be done at four points throughout the day, thus giving us a better idea of our pattern of diurnal cortisol. This method of collection is non-invasive and convenient, and several studies suggest that it gives a more accurate evaluation of the level of the cortisol being used by the body.

The drawback to this testing method is that the results can be affected by contamination of the blood through such instances as gingivitis or aggressive brushing or with certain oral medications. Therefore, close attention must be paid to the collection instructions.

Another valuable way to get an idea of the daily production of stress hormones is to measure the levels in urine that has been collected over 24 consecutive hours. This method is non-invasive and accurate. The limitations include the fact that it is only as accurate as collection consistency. In other words, you can't miss collection of any urine in that period. This method is also unable to show diurnal variation, or various fluctuations that occur throughout the day.

## Nutritional Factors

Another key area to evaluate when it comes to the anxiety response is the assessment of your nutritional status. After all, food and proper nutrition fuel our bodies and our brains. A basic laboratory evaluation would rule out contributing nutritional factors such as anemia, iron deficiency (which is not the same thing, as discussed below), or abnormal blood sugar or mineral levels such as calcium, magnesium and potassium.

Anemia can sometimes present as a panic attack, as the heart is working harder and pumping faster to make up for the lack of red blood cells. If anemia is present, then your physician's next step would be to determine what is causing the anemia in the first place.

Iron deficiency is one cause of anemia, but many times people seem to use the term anemia and iron deficiency synonymously. This is not the case. While iron deficiency can create anemia, not all

146

anemia is secondary to iron deficiency. Besides creating anemia in your body, being iron deficient could also affect your moods as well.

That's because iron deficiency can cause unexplained fatigue, lack of focus and even contribute to depression. One of the reasons that this may occur is that iron plays a significant role in the formation of neurotransmitters such as norepinephrine and dopamine.

Other causes of anemia and mood disorders include being deficient in vitamin B-12 and folic acid. In lab studies, vitamin B-12 has been shown to protect the neurons from toxicity caused by the excess of the excitatory amino acid glutamate. Research has also found that folic acid deficiency has been associated with lower serotonin levels, perhaps offering a mechanism by which folic acid could contribute to improving mood disorders.

This theory is supported by the numerous studies that show that the effects of anti-depressants were improved with the addition of folic acid in the user's diet. Numerous studies have associated vitamin D with an increased risk for mood disorders, so checking a patient's level to ensure optimal levels may be helpful.

Research suggests that vitamin D may play a role in down regulating the HPA axis, thus modulating cortisol levels as well. Other research suggests that it may also play a role in regulating the receptors for brain derived neurotropic factor (BDNF), the chemical that nurtures and protects nerve cells.

## The Mystery of "Functional Deficiencies"

While no one disputes the significance of obtaining the absolute value of these nutrients, there is some discussion about the value of what are known as functional deficiencies. Functional deficiencies are defined as deficiencies that are strongly suspected, due to symptomatology, despite "normal" laboratory values. In other words, while the absolute value laboratory evidence may be to the contrary, the physical evidence or symptomatology points towards nutrient deficiency and should prompt one to further explore functional deficiencies.

If one examines normal ranges closely, especially for nutrient values, one would note the wide range that is considered "normal."

For example, the normal range for vitamin B12 in most labs ranges between an average of 200 and 900pcg/ml. The question is often asked, "What is the optimal range?" In other words, what is the range that helps an individual function at his or her best? What is the range that helps to maintain optimal energy, clarity of thinking and peak performance and is there a way to identify this value?

Reputable nutritional labs, such as Genova Diagnostics and Metametrix, insist there is such a way to identify this optimal value. In fact, they have spent much time and scientific research delving into this very question. One way they have provided the practitioner with the ability to understand this number better is by closely studying a constellation of urine organic acids or other byproducts in the urine.

These acids are produced in specific amounts by the various metabolic processes in our body, which are oftentimes dependent on the nutrients being present in optimal amounts. Too much or too little of these urine organic acids could indicate a functional deficiency of a particular nutrient or a dysfunction in that particular pathway.

A good example of this that is traditionally used is vitamin B-12. If a deficiency is suspected, but its absolute value is determined to be normal through routine testing, then physicians will go on to measure a substance known as methylmalonic acid. Why? This is because an elevation in this byproduct is indicative of vitamin B-12 deficiency, regardless of the original "normal" reading.

Likewise, a urine organic level evaluation will look at functional deficiencies of other nutrients such as vitamin B-6, vitamin C and folic acid, to name just a few.

Another benefit of this test is a screening evaluation of proper bacterial balance in the gut, so here we have the proverbial two birds with one stone – and a real breakthrough in determining biological root causes of anxiety-producing symptoms that might otherwise be missed during "routine" testing.

| Nutrient Deficiencies | Effects |
|---|---|
| **Vitamin B-6** | Can affect levels of GABA (calming) and serotonin |
| **Vitamin B-12** | Protects neurons from an early death from high levels of glutamate (excitatory) |
| **Vitamin B-3** | May favor production of serotonin from L-Tryptophan<br><br>May help to decrease lactic acid, which can trigger anxiety |
| **Magnesium** | Works to improve efficacy of cognitive therapy<br><br>Improves memory<br><br>Can provide feeling of relaxation |
| **Omega-3** | Shown to decrease inflammation<br><br>May improve symptoms of anxiety |
| **Vitamin D** | May help to balance cortisol levels<br><br>Helps BDNF (helps to protect neurons and improve moods) receptor to work better<br><br>Modulates the immune system, thus possibly inflammation |
| **Folate** | Low levels associated with lower levels of serotonin<br><br>Improves function of anti-depressants |

**Figure 7.1:** *Nutrient Deficiencies and Their Physical Effects.*

**Further Testing for Targeted Treatment**

Your physician may also want to take a sneak peek at your inflammatory status by looking at the levels of your C-reactive protein (CRP). Studies show that this level correlates well with the levels of pro-inflammatory cytokines in the body. Therefore, an elevation of CRP would point toward elevation of cytokines and inflammation as well.

Such testing often leads to strange bedfellows in the remedy department. In this case, for instance, treatment of inflammation may then be a part of your anti-anxiety plan (believe it or not!).

The measurement of arachidonic acid and omega-3 ratio may also be a screening tool to help determine if an imbalance in good – or anti-inflammatory – fats versus bad – or pro-inflammatory – fats is contributing to your symptoms. Arachidonic acid is an inflammatory fatty acid that is produced when cell membranes (including neurons) are damaged and broken down.

Research has recently revealed that activation of the NMDA receptors causes an increase in the enzyme that breaks down cell membranes (phospholipase A). This, in turn, can cause an elevation in arachidonic acid. Thus, an elevation in this inflammatory fatty acid could indicate an overactivation of the NMDA receptors. Also, low levels of omega-3 anti-inflammatory fatty acid could make it difficult to maximize the results of anti-anxiety treatment.

If gut involvement is suspected from symptoms and/or the urine organic acid evaluation, then a comprehensive stool analysis may be in order. This type of thorough stool analysis not only identifies potential pathogens, but also looks at inflammatory markers, i.e., markers for optimal digestion and the presence of adequate "good" (i.e., healthy) bacteria.

**Origin of Species:** *Where – And When – Did the Anxiety Begin?*

This is all well and good, from your doctor's perspective, but what about you? What can *you* control, personally speaking? In other words, what if the food you eat is actually contributing to your anxiety symptoms?

Well, if your doctor suspects that inflammation due to food sensitivity is fueling the anxiety, then a food sensitivity evaluation may be the next logical step in the diagnosis process. After all, there is little point in attempting to repair the gut if it is continually being challenged, worn down and compromised by foods that produce a significant immune response.

From the discussions in the previous chapters it would seem that managing anxiety requires a multi-pronged approach. It would also seem that anxiety may be a learned, hyper-reactive response triggered in susceptible individuals and fueled by inflammation and chemical imbalance.

In other words, you may have come to your current, anxious state in a predetermined way that was confounded, year by year, by physical reactions that were equally out of your control! Yet here you are, a "victim" – for lack of a better term – of your own body!

So, one of the more confounding parts about this disorder is that we may not recall where or when we learned it in the first place. Ask yourself: Can you pinpoint when you started feeling, let alone acting, anxious? Can you determine a day and date when all this "started"? If you're like many of my patients, the answer is probably "no."

Studies are even suggesting that in some cases the origins of anxiety may be in the perinatal period or early childhood, in which case, we may never remember the precipitating event(s) that led to our anxious feelings!

Other studies provocatively suggest that anxiety can be triggered, not by an emotional event or trauma, as one might expect, but rather by an infection or even the wrong type of bacteria in the gut. So, like an emotional scar that may take years to heal, infections on or in our gut could be damaging more than just our body, but our mind as well.

Regardless of the cause, physical or mental, or even the origin, early or late onset, most studies seem to agree, regardless of the trigger, the behavioral response is controlled by the brain.

That is why most anxiety pharmaceutical medications have been targeted at the brain, its neurotransmitters and their receptors. While I agree that this is indeed the biggest target and, perhaps, even the one with the most immediate response, my professional – and clinical – position is that we should also be simultaneously attempting to remove or at least lessen the wind from fanning the flames so the brain stands a better chance of responding to treatment.

## Cognitive Behavioral Therapy and the Brain

Cognitive behavioral therapy (CBT) is a form of therapy that helps one to become aware of their behaviors and learn strategies to manage these patterns around anxiety and stress. A review of efficacy of cognitive behavioral therapy published in the *Journal of Clinical Psychiatry* in 2008 looked at 27 studies done on CBT and anxiety and came to the conclusion that it was, indeed, an effective treatment modality.

Cognitive behavioral therapy is based on the process of fear reduction, or elimination. Studies suggest that the very receptors (NMDA-R) that, if overstimulated in certain areas of the brain (such as the amygdala), create anxiety, are also important in the learned extinction of that anxiety or fear.

If we think of fear as a highly adaptive form of learning that helps to keep us safe, then we can better understand how learning a different response to fear signals (such as occurs in cognitive behavioral therapy) can involve activating the same receptors that are involved in the acquisition of the very fear we are trying to avoid.

To support this theory, studies using a medication called D-cycloserine, which activates (or acts as an "agonist" for) the NMDA receptors, administered about an hour prior to fear extinction therapy made the therapy more effective. Also, if chemicals designed to block the activation of the NMDA receptors were given either prior to or following the fear extinction therapy, then therapy did not work as well and, as a result, the fear remained.

Further experiments suggest that while the amygdala is important in the initial response to therapy to reduce fear, it is actually the prefrontal cortex (cognitive) that is responsible for continuing to remind the amygdala to keep the fear response in check. Again, this is the brain working in concert with various hormonal "checks and balances" to optimize function.

Animal studies show that early perinatal trauma (i.e., shortly after birth) can actually decrease our ability to respond positively to cognitive therapy and that medications like SSRI (anti-depressant) and D-cycloserine can restore the brain's ability to respond well to therapy. So, in our quest to find the right drug, or even herb, to treat anxiety, we must not forget that we need to teach the brain what we want it to learn.

**Neurofeedback and the Brain**

As mentioned in the previous chapter, neurofeedback, while in its infancy, has shown promise in many studies in the treatment of anxiety. It may augment cognitive therapy as well. Studies also support its use for increasing focus and some suggest it may be beneficial as an adjunct to help to treat insomnia, an enemy to effective anti-anxiety treatment.

I have seen some my patients benefit significantly when using this therapy as part of their anxiety treatment plan. A brief word of caution: this is still a new field, so it is important that you work with your physician to find a reputable, trained practitioner before beginning this type of therapy.

**Exercise and the Brain**

What if I told you that you can actually *regrow* nerve cells in your brain? Well, you can! Given that truism, would you also believe that it doesn't require a magic pill or even an herb? It only requires that you exercise.

That's right! Studies show that physical exercise can actually remodel the brain and promote the growth of new neurons, especially in the areas of the brain responsible for memory. Initial studies in this field were performed on mice and it was shown that they were able to grow new nerve cells in the hippocampus, the region of the brain associated with memory.

Researchers were able to correlate this increase in neurogenesis, or nerve growth, in rodents by mapping increased blood volume circulating to the areas of new growth. Using this technique, researchers at Columbia University were able to demonstrate that exercise has similar effects on the human brain.

Using functional MRI they were able to demonstrate a significant increase in blood flow to the same areas of the brain corresponding to memory as originally occurred in the mice, thus suggesting that new nerves were being formed under the influence of exercise.

To further support the beneficial effect that exercise has on the brain, several studies show a direct link between exercise and the increase in BNDF, that growth factor that has been shown to be responsible for the health and growth of neurons as well as playing an integral role in maintaining psychological well-being.

Remember, for any therapy or treatment approach to work – be it chemical- or cognitive-based – you must have a healthy, functioning brain and, if your physician recommends exercise as part of your treatment plan, this could be why.

## Herbs and the Brain

But, exercise isn't the only "natural" cure for anxiety and the stress response. There are actually several herbs that, in studies, have been shown to have an effect on the brain and its neurotransmitters. Each has a slightly different mechanism of action and exhibited good safety profiles in these studies.

Many are easy to locate, either over the counter or in health food stores. I will list the various herbs in question, as well as a brief user profile for each below:

1. **Valerian officianalis** – is a plant native to Europe and Asia. It has a distinctive odor that many interpret as unpleasant. It is the dried root and the stems of this herb that are used for medicinal purposes. Several small studies have found valerian effective for treatment of mild anxiety. Research suggests that valerian (or valerian "root" as it is often referred to) can activate GABA (calming) receptors while blocking the glutamate (excitatory receptors). Other studies suggest that valerian may be more effective in combination with other herbs better known for their calming properties, such as chamomile and lemon balm. One study found the combination

to be more effective in lower doses, so more is not necessarily better in this case. Due to the sedative nature of the herb, it should not be combined with sedative medications unless under the supervision of your physician. In studies, valerian demonstrated a good safety profile when taken in the recommended dosages.

2. **L-Theanine** – is an amino acid extracted from green tea. In studies it has been shown to activate the GABA-A receptors to produce a calming effect. Studies show that it may also have effects on other neurotransmitters as well, such as dopamine and serotonin. L-Theanine has been shown in animal studies to protect neurons from injury during decreased blood flow to the brain (simulating a stroke), thereby aiding in the recovery of neurons when blood flow was returned. Research also reveals that L-Theanine has the ability to decrease the conversion of the amino acid glutamine to the excitatory neurotransmitter glutamate. Remember, glutamate in excess

has been shown to be toxic to nerve cells. Finally, L-Theanine has been shown in studies to increase alpha waves in the brain. As you recall, alpha waves are the dominant waves during mental and physical relaxation. L-Theanine has a very high safety profile.

3. **Passion Flower (*Passiflora incarnate*)** – A double-blind randomized study comparing passion flower and a prescription anti-anxiety medication in the benzodiazepine group showed that passion flower was just as effective as this medication, but with fewer sedative side effects.

4. **Apigenin** – This little known herb is actually a flavonoid found in dried chamomile flowers that has been shown to have anti-anxiety properties. Research supports that apigenin works by reducing the response in the NMDA receptors to overstimulation by the neurotransmitter glutamate and, therefore, reduces the excitability of the neuron.

5. **Kava (Piper methysticum)** – is a plant native to the Polynesian islands. The herb is derived from the root of the plant only, as the aerial parts and stems contain potentially toxic substances. Even then, the aqueous extract standardized for kavalactones, not to exceed 250mg daily, is the recommended way to take this herb. Kava does have a wide variety of studies that have shown efficacy in reducing anxiety symptoms. Warning: cases of liver injury have been reported while using Kava. It seems in some cases the inappropriate form was used, and other substances may have been implicated as well. I would recommend caution when using this herb and, if using this herb, work closely with your physician. It should be avoided in people with a history of liver disorders or who are on other medications that could potentially affect the liver, such as statins. The mechanism of action has not been fully elucidated but a GABA effect is suspected.

6. **Tryptophan** – is the essential amino acid that is converted to serotonin, the neurotransmitter thought to play a significant role in the treatment of anxiety symptoms. Studies show that depletion of tryptophan actually increases symptoms of anxiety. One study using food high in tryptophan combined with carbohydrates showed improvement in anxiety symptoms. I feel one word of caution is necessary before we continue our discussion: the use of l-tryptophan in individuals with high cortisol levels or excessive inflammation could produce inflammatory byproducts that could potentially stimulate NMDA receptors, thus potentially increasing anxiety.

Many of these herbs may be new to you, but I include them here because science has proven them effective in the natural, holistic fight against stress and the anxiety response.

**Nutrients and the Brain**

For our neurons and neurotransmitters to function normally, the body needs to be replete in the proper nutrients that play a significant role in the brain's optimal function. The following are specific nutrients that have been tied to optimal brain function:

1. **Vitamin B-6** plays an important role in the formation of two of the key neurotransmitters implicated in anxiety: serotonin and GABA. Several studies, looking at premenstrual depression and anxiety, showed an improvement in symptoms with vitamin B-6 alone or in combination with magnesium. Also known as pyridoxine (most common form found in vitamins), vitamin B-6 is converted in the liver to the metabolically active enzyme pyridoxal-5-phosphate (P5P). This form of B-6 is the only form that can be used in reactions in the body, so the form found in most vitamins must first be converted by the liver prior to use. Studies have suggested that using P5P in individuals who are deficient in vitamin B-6 would be more effective than using pyridoxine HCL.

2.  **Magnesium** has been shown in several studies to improve not only the general symptoms of anxiety, but also to enhance the effects of cognitive therapy. Magnesium is involved in more than 300 chemical reactions in the body, and one of its functions is modulating the NMDA receptor. As you'll recall, this is the receptor that is important in learning, whether you are learning to acquire a fear response or, in our case, learning to undo it!

3.  **Vitamin B-12** has been shown to protect nerve cells from damage. In the lab, nerve cells that were bathed in vitamin B-12 were protected from injury when an overabundance of the excitatory neurotransmitter glutamate was introduced. One study looking at 1,000 young, healthy males found that those who had borderline vitamin B-12 deficiency exhibited more symptoms of anxiety.

4. **Niacinamide (Vitamin B-3)**. About one percent of the niacin made in the body is derived from the amino acid L-tryptophan. One study suggested that the niacinamide form of Vitamin B-3 may have effects similar to the anti-anxiety medicines in the benzodiazepine family. Niacin is also thought to have an effect on increasing serotonin production by favoring the metabolism of tryptophan toward serotonin, instead of toward the other inflammatory products that tryptophan also produces.

5. **Lactate.** Elevated lactate levels have been shown to induce anxiety. Lactate is produced during the processing of glucose into energy (ATP). Heavy exercise and decreased oxygen levels can induce lactic acid formation. Niacin has been shown to reduce lactate levels. Several case studies have reported reduction in anxiety with the use of niacinamide. While I am not aware of any double-blind placebo studies, the above mechanisms of action could certainly support an anxiolytic

effect. As some reports suggest that niacinamide can potentially cause an adverse reaction on the liver and on blood sugar levels, I recommend using niacinamide (Vitamin B-3) in consultation with your physician.

6. **Myo-inositol** is considered a B-vitamin. It can be synthesized in the body from glucose. It is not currently considered an essential nutrient because most of it can be synthesized in the human kidney at a rate of a few grams day. This has brought into question whether it should be classified as a vitamin in the first place. Several studies have shown that myo-inositol improved anxiety and depressive symptoms with high safety profile and minimal side effects. In fact, one study found it to be just as effective as an SSRI (for Selective Serotonin Re-uptake Inhibitor, which works on serotonin) for anxiety. A double-blind placebo study also showed that it improved ovarian function in women suffering from PCOS. Additionally, individuals in the myo-inositol group lost a

significant amount of weight when compared to the placebo group. Inositol is thought to modulate the cells' response to serotonin. From its action on ovaries, it may play a role in hormonal balancing as well.

Again, be they herbal or nutritional/vitamin supplements, the above lists are designed to offer you a variety of holistic, nutritional options to help alleviate some of your anxiety-related symptoms. In all cases, consult your treating physician before diving headfirst into the world of supplements.

## The Better You Eat, the Fewer Supplements You Need to Take

Another important part of keeping the brain healthy is an all-around healthy nutritional plan. I'm not necessarily talking about nutritional supplements, like we did in the previous two sections, but instead I'm referring to how you eat, daily, on a habitual basis.

While we often speak of how bad certain foods are for you, and with good reason, we don't often enough dwell on the positive effects certain diets, even specific foods, can have on our overall and cognitive health, particularly when it comes to stress and anxiety.

For example, research supports that the Mediterranean diet, high in fruits, vegetables, whole grains, fish and unsaturated fats, can help maintain healthy brain function and reduce the risk of depression and cognitive decline.

Foods that are high in anti-oxidant value, such as berries, have been shown to support healthy brain function as well. The brain has an extremely high metabolic rate and, as a result, produces a lot of free radicals (which many studies relate to advanced aging). Oxidative stress has been correlated with a lot of chronic diseases, including decreased cognition and increased risk for neurodegeneration.

Foods that contain polyunsaturated and monounsaturated fats, such as avocadoes and olive oil, have been shown to promote healthy brain function while foods high in trans-fats (processed foods) and saturated fats have the opposite effect. Remember, a healthy brain requires healthy nerve cells (neurons) and healthy neurons are needed for any intervention to work effectively.

These are just a variety of ways in which what you eat can affect how you feel, and even how you behave. Take some time to research more specific nutrition options and how they can reduce your stress, which could mean a few trips to the library or even Amazon.com to begin delving more deeply into the food you eat and how it makes you feel!

**Protect Your Head; Reduce Your Stress!**

Another component of any healthy brain program is to protect your brain from injury and trauma. Studies now support significant neurological sequelae from Chronic Traumatic Brain Injury. This repetitive injury can occur with sports such as soccer, football and boxing.

A study published in *JAMA*, or the *Journal of the American Medical Association*, suggested that the extent of the symptoms correlate with the frequency of the head trauma. In other words, the more often the injury occurred, say in a professional boxer or football player, the more significant the symptoms.

This study also suggests that individuals with a certain genotype (*APOE* ∈4 allele) exposed to frequent head trauma are at increased risk for more severe neurological deficits.

Treatment for this type of brain injury is very much in its infancy and, therefore, prevention is the best cure. This could include such simple tasks as:

- **Wearing a helmet while bicycling, skating, etc.**

- **Monitoring the sports you and your children play.**

- **Investing in the proper equipment for contact sports (i.e., helmets, pads, padding, mouthpieces, etc.)**

While I am not personally aware of studies that specifically tie anxiety to repeated brain trauma, healthy neurons are required for a healthy brain, so the connection seems quite clear. Also, trauma has a negative impact on healthy brainwave patterns.

**Managing the Hypothalamic Pituitary Adrenal Axis and Stress in Anxiety:** *Modalities for Treatment*

It is important to manage and address the HPA axis in the stress response. Remember, this response is the brain's direct connection to the body to produce the fight or flight response. Consider it the brain's freeway to anxiety! And, if you'll recall, there are many things that can activate this system, such as norepinephrine from the locus coeruleus, inflammatory cytokines produced from infection or inflammation, and external traumatic or stressful events.

In a previous section we discussed measuring cortisol levels as one way to gauge the stress response in the body, and the different forms of measurements available to modern medicine, as well as their pros and cons. Interestingly enough, heart rate variability (HRV) may be another new way to measure the brain's connection to the body and the heart.

Let's revisit the chain reaction that leads to actual feelings of stress in your body: first, the brain activates the adrenal glands. Next up, the stress hormones, cortisol and adrenaline, have an impact on

174

the autonomic nervous system, which then has an impact on the heart and blood vessels. Remember that high levels of adrenaline can cause blood vessels to constrict, including blood vessels to the heart.

This squeezing of the blood vessels may in fact be one of the factors that contribute to low heart rate variability (HRV) and increased risk of heart disease and sudden cardiac death. Recall also that low heart rate variability is associated with anxiety and depression.

But, all is not lost, and there are treatments available to help reduce these effects. In fact, I've included several such modalities below that may be helpful in controlling the HPA response and, therefore, controlling the anxiety response. One way to monitor the effectiveness of these techniques may be to monitor HRV

***Stress management strategies such as exercise and meditation***

Never underestimate the power of natural, even instinctual, acts like movement and meditation to curb your stress. A study out of the University of Maryland School of Public Health showed that 30 minutes of moderate exercise reduced anxiety as well as 30 minute of relaxation.

However, those individuals who exercised regularly were able to maintain the reduced anxiety levels even when exposed to anxiety-provoking stimuli. The rest group did not seem to maintain that benefit.

A recent study comparing the benefits of yoga versus relaxation techniques in management of anxiety found that both were equally effective. This study also discovered benefits in blood pressure management as well. What's important to take away from this study is how the group that exercised didn't just receive immediate benefits of reduced anxiety, but were better able to deflect, i.e., avoid, the deleterious effects of stress even when they were finished exercising. This makes a strong case for moving more often, and making regular exercise – along with proper nutrition – a habitual behavior.

While movement has been proven to reduce anxiety symptoms, so has the lack of movement – in this case, meditation.

Meditation has been shown to increase heart rate variability and help to calm the mind and body. It has also been shown to increase parasympathetic tone, thus decreasing heart rate.

Heart rate increases when we inhale and decreases when we exhale. As you may or may not know, meditative practices focus on releasing air through a long exhalation process, thus helping to reduce heart rate and produce a calming effect on both the body and mind.

Of course, one does not have to meditate to benefit from this technique. Taking just a few minutes several times a day, or before a potentially stressful event, to focus on exhaling can provide similar calming/anxiety-reducing benefits.

### Try the "hand warming" technique

Another strategy that may be helpful is often referred to as the "hand warming" technique. You may notice that at times of high stress and anxiety, your hands often become colder than during non-stressful times. This is a secondary effect due to the blood vessels in the hands being constricted, thus shunting blood away from the hands to the larger muscles in preparation for fight of flight.

So, what can we do about it? Performing an exercise to open up and relax the blood vessels to the hands, causing them to re-warm, may also be relaxing other blood vessels in the process, such as those arteries supplying the heart. In fact, some studies show that this technique can indeed create a decrease in blood pressure.

To practice this simple "hand warming" technique, start by taking 5-10 deep breaths. Close your eyes and imagine yourself holding your hands over a warming fire, or even holding a hot cup of your favorite tea or coffee. Imagine, or "feel," the warmth seep into your hands slowly. Feel or visualize the blood vessels in your hands opening up and allowing the blood to return to your hands.

With practice, some people are able to increase the temperature in their hands by several degrees. Attaching a digit thermometer to your fingers may help you to record the temperature change as you grow in proficiency with this practice.

### *Consider therapy with essential oils*

Several essential oils have been shown to be effective in soothing the anxiety response. For example, in studies lavender essential oil has been demonstrated to activate the parasympathetic nervous system to create a calming response. Studies also found that it was able to calm the anxiety associated with dementia in the elderly.

Another study looking at an oral form of lavender essential oil, silexan, showed efficacy comparable to the prescription anti-anxiety medicines in the benzodiazepine family. If you recall, the parasympathetic system is part of the autonomic nervous system and it creates a balance with the sympathetic nervous system.

Stress and anxiety tend to activate the sympathetic nervous system, thus increasing heart rate, feelings of anxiousness, shakiness, etc. The parasympathetic system can create a feeling of calm by reducing heart rate and improving motility of gut and digestion, thus decreasing feelings of nausea and those "butterflies in stomach" we all know so well. (And some of you reading this book know all *too* well!)

Keep in mind that these two systems are always active; it is the balance between them that is important when it comes to understanding, and reducing, the anxiety response.

### *Massage Therapy*

Most of us would agree that even a 10-minute massage can start relieving some of the tension we carry in our bodies on a daily basis and we can actually start feeling ourselves relax almost immediately. You may be interested to know that massage therapy is much more than an indulgence, to be enjoyed during a weekend getaway or luxury spa day. It actually has the ability to change our biochemistry.

In 2005, *The International Journal of Neuroscience* published a review of several studies that looked at changes in the body after massage therapy. The majority of studies showed that massage therapy actually decreased the levels of the stress hormone cortisol, while increasing serotonin and dopamine levels – thus improving our moods and decreasing anxiety.

So, the next time your spouse suggests you take a spa day or you drive by an alternative health center featuring a deep tissue massage, don't just reject it out of hand. Instead, look at it as a potential form of therapy for the stress symptoms that have been plaguing you.

### Magnolia officinalis

The bark of the magnolia tree is thought to contain at least two active ingredients with the potential to reduce symptoms of the anxiety response. In studies these two extracts, honokiol and magnolol, have been shown to have anti-anxiety properties.

These extracts seem to exert their dual action on the hypothalamic pituitary adrenal axis. In animal studies, they have been proven to decrease the production of corticosterone, the equivalent to cortisol in the human body. This then decreases the effects that excess cortisol may have on the body. Other mechanisms of actions suggested in these studies include an increase in serotonin levels and decrease in the inflammatory cytokines that can stimulate the anxiety response.

## Sex Hormones, the Brain and Moods

To recap the material presented so far, we have already noted the potentially beneficial neurobiological effects of hormones such as estrogen, testosterone and progesterone on the brain and subsequent moods experienced as a result of those hormones.

Specifically, estrogen has been shown to reduce anxiety, improve depression and enhance memory. Estrogen's effects in the brain seem to be mediated by the alpha estrogen receptors. Testosterone has a similar effect in males and females in that a deficiency has been correlated with increased anxiety. In males, it also seems to have an anti-depressant effect.

If hormonal deficiency is suspected to be contributing in any way to your mood disorders, then checking hormonal levels should be part of your medical evaluation. There are several ways to evaluate hormonal levels. As previously discussed, these include using serum, saliva or urine samples to establish deficiency or excess.

Urine samples can include spot urine collection, or a 24-hour collection that gives an idea of the entire day's production of hormones. Saliva samples are more convenient and less invasive to collect. Some studies support the use of a saliva specimen because it is thought to represent only the bioactive, or "free," amounts of hormones. There are, however, ongoing brisk discussions about the reproducibility or reliability of these results. Each of these collection methods has its supporters and detractors.

Personally, I like to use 24-hour urine collection because I believe it gives a more detailed look at the production for the entire day, thus minimizing the cyclical variation (or up and down spikes, peaks and valleys) that can occur throughout the day.

Regardless of the collection method, it is important to pay attention to both your symptoms and the lab work together, and **not** **just the lab work**. For example, if you are undergoing hormonal therapy and making adjustments to your regimen using one method of testing, and yet your symptoms are worsening while the lab work is improving, you may want to ask your physician to check your levels using an alternate collection method. He or she may find that this alternate method more accurately reflects your symptoms than the traditional collection methods they've been using. (As a side note, your symptoms are very powerful reminders of what *you* are feeling and should always be considered!)

For males, it is recommended that the specimen be collected in the morning, as that is the time that testosterone peaks. Because women's hormonal levels are more cyclical, more attention needs to be paid to the time in her menstrual cycle that the specimen was collected. For example, estrogen levels will be more dominant in the first half of the cycle and progesterone levels will be minimal.

Progesterone levels start to increase about halfway through the cycle and peaks about a week later. Knowing when the specimen was collected is helpful when interpreting the results. Many experts believe that the best time to get a snapshot is between days 19-21 of a cycle in order to get an idea of peak levels of all hormones.

The figure on the next page provides a "snapshot" view of this cycle in visual form:

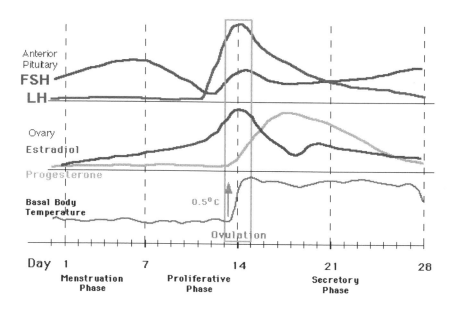

**Figure 7.2:** *A snapshot of the Menstruation, Proliferative and Secretory Phases.*

Despite the beneficial effects of these hormones on reducing stress and the anxiety response, there are many aspects that need to be taken into consideration prior to instituting hormonal therapy. Recent studies strongly suggest that administering estrogen long after menopause can actually increase risk of strokes and even adversely affect memory.

One animal study in particular, performed by Dr. Darrell Braun and presented at Proceedings of National Academy of Sciences, offers a mechanism of action by which this occurs. It would appear that if neuron receptors in the brain are deprived of estrogen for an extended period of time, the CHIP (carboxyl terminus of HSC70 interacting protein) enzyme binds to these receptors and has them taken off to be destroyed. If estrogen therapy is introduced after this development occurs, then there is an increased occurrence of strokes.

So far, studies suggest that, when it comes to neurological protection, the most beneficial time for estrogen therapy is right at menopause and no later than two to three years after the event. So, a word of caution: if you are 10 years postmenopausal and have not had any replacement therapy in that time, then estrogen replacement therapy may actually increase your risk of strokes and negatively impact your brain health. You and your treating physician will want to examine whether the benefits of hormone therapy in regards to reducing your stress outweigh the stroke risks involved in treatment.

Furthermore, introducing hormones this late post-menopausal does not seem to decrease risk of Alzheimer's or improve memory. I am also not aware of any studies that have examined if a similar mechanism is at play with male hormonal replacement therapy with testosterone and if there is an optimal time to replace testosterone.

## Pharmaceuticals and the Brain

Now, I know many of you are wondering if there isn't just a simple pharmaceutical fix for anxiety. With the advancements made in modern medicine these days, there are indeed some pharmaceuticals specifically targeted to help control excessive anxiety response.

The two primary pharmacological interventions used to treat anxiety are medications targeted at the GABA and serotonin receptors in the brain, and we will also discuss the use of beta blockers in the pharmaceutical treatment of stress.

## *Serotonin Boosters*

The most commonly used serotonin boosters are anti-depressants referred to as SSRI (selective serotonin reuptake inhibitors). Their actions elevate the levels of serotonin in the brain by preventing their reuptake by the neurons that break down and recycle these neurotransmitters.

This reaction then makes more serotonin available to exert its inhibitory effect, thus creating a calming response. Other SSRIs act on specific serotonin receptors to produce a serotonin calming effect. You and your physician can work to determine which, if any, of the SSRI is appropriate for you.

I feel a few words of caution are in order as we begin to discuss the more pharmaceutical remedies for stress. Case in point: long-term use of SSRI-type medications have been linked with decreased bone mass, thus increasing the risk of osteoporosis. Therefore, if you and your doctor are considering the use of SSRIs, then paying attention to bone health along the way would be prudent.

Another concern I feel it important to note here is that studies show that after long-term use of SSRIs, the level of serotonin in the brain becomes lower than the baseline, or starting, serotonin levels. Oftentimes the individual being treated may feel at that time that the medication has "stopped working."

Anti-depressants can also decrease libido and, at times, create a "flat" affect, emotionally speaking. Many people describe this feeling as neither being happy or sad, just not feeling much of anything at all. Oftentimes this is treated with the addition of another anti-depressant with a different mechanism of action to offset this feeling. However, this leads many patients to discontinue their use of the anti-depressant. In effect, many of them would rather risk feeling anxious and stressed again than, well, not feeling anything at all.

The flipside of the coin includes the fact that several studies have shown a link between reduced risk of primary occurrence of colorectal cancer and long term SSRI use. There have been some concerns expressed about an increase in the occurrence of breast and ovarian cancer with the use of anti-depressants as well.

Those studies appeared to be inconclusive, however, with some showing an increased link but the majority showing no link whatsoever. The studies that seem to be the most consistent are those that link SSRI use with an increased risk of recurrence of breast cancer in survivors also taking tamoxifen. These studies also showed an increased risk of dying from breast cancer.

While the safety profile of SSRI over their predecessors tricyclic anti-depressants and MAOI inhibitors have been noted, overdose of these medications can produce what is known as "serotonin syndrome." Symptoms of serotonin syndrome can range from confusion, agitation, headaches, nausea and diarrhea to muscle twitching, palpitations, seizures and unconsciousness, so as with any prescription medication, take only as prescribed and notify your physician immediately with any changes.

### GABA (gamma aminobutyric acid) Boosters

The most commonly used gamma aminobutyric acid (GABA) receptors booster medications belong to a class of drugs known as benzodiazepine. The ideal indication for these medications, in my opinion, is the short-term use for relief of significant anxiety. For example, they may be started at the same time as an anti-depressant for severe symptoms, as anti-depressants take up to four to six weeks to attain full effect. Benzodiazepines have been shown to be effective in many studies.

There is one major issue that rears its head again and again when it comes to GABA boosters, and that is the significantly increased risk of addictive behaviors. Also, many people on this class of medication can exhibit an increase in disinhibited risk-taking behaviors.

This class of drug can also be extremely sedating, thus increasing risks of accidents and decreasing productivity. They have also been shown to increase risk of dementia in elderly patients. Again, anyone seeking a permanent solution to their anxiety symptoms should view the use of GABA boosters realistically, as in my opinion short-term use is best.

## *Beta Blockers*

Imagine if a prescription drug could essentially interrupt, or "block," the anxiety response. Well, as the name implies, beta blockers are sometimes used to block the sympathetic response that is created when the anxiety pathway is activated. They have been shown to be effective in public speaking phobias as well other acute anxiety states. Some studies suggest that beta blockers are more effective when combined with other anti-anxiety medications.

Again, a necessary caveat: Beta blockers can induce depression in susceptible individuals, so it is recommended that they not be used in patients experiencing anxiety when there is also depression present.

There are other medications used in the treatment of anxiety, such as anti-seizure and anti-psychotic medicines, that are beyond the scope of this book (which is intended for general audiences and not as a diagnosis for severe anxiety symptoms).

If your anxiety symptom is overwhelming and unrelenting, there is a possibility that you might be dealing with another psychological disorder and you should work closely with your physician and perhaps psychiatrist to get to the root of the problem.

**Case Study:** *Jennifer*

After reading her latest results, I noted that Jennifer's neurotransmitter test suggested that her serotonin level was low. Her eating patterns were off as well, so her brain was most likely being deprived of essential nutrients.

She exercised sporadically, so Jennifer was not reaping the benefits of regular exercise which, as we've seen, were shown to provide both short- and long-term stress-reducing effects. She avoided another natural stress reducer, massage therapy, because she complained that "it took too long."

A low cortisol level was signifying significant stress that was beginning to take its toll on Jennifer's body. Her issue with insomnia was further fueling the fire. Not only was her sporadic eating preventing her body from getting the nutrients it needed, but to make matters worse her insomnia was preventing her body from getting the sleep it so desperately needed.

My plan for Jennifer included focusing on improving her eating habits, for starters. We mapped out a plan to eat four to five small meals a day to help to maintain steady blood sugar levels. Part of Jennifer's problem was that she was becoming hypoglycemic, and this was contributing to her anxiety.

We incorporated vegetables for antioxidant value, and then added omega-3 foods such as fish, nuts and other quality proteins to provide building blocks for essential neurotransmitters. I then taught Jennifer brief relaxation exercises, such as the hand warming technique we learned in this chapter, to perform at moments throughout the day whenever she started to feel overwhelmed. She also agreed to incorporate a 10-15 minute chair massage once a week for the following month.

To support her cortisol level without hyperstimulation, I added high-dose vitamin C with a B-complex that focused on vitamins B6/B5/B12/Folate. To address her issues with insomnia, low serotonin and low magnesium, I added a chamomile/lemon balm tea with inositol and magnesium. I also asked her to do a brief affirmation before going to bed and first thing when she awoke in the morning. It simply stated: "I have nothing to fear. I am safe and protected at all times."

On her two-week follow up, Jennifer was feeling much better. She stated that her level of anxiety had significantly improved and her energy level was returning to normal. The only issue she reported was that there were some nights that she still experienced some issues falling asleep.

To help stave off the encroaching insomnia, we added a small dose of L-Tryptophan at night for one week and thereafter as needed. She called the next week to report that she felt she was well on her way to feeling her normal self, so much so that she started back on her regular exercise routine.

# Chapter 8:

## *Quench Inflammation to Improve Your Moods & Overall Health*

At this point in our journey together, I would hope that you're familiar enough with the causes of anxiety to be both prepared for, and eager to get to, its treatment. And thus we begin by talking about inflammation and the role it can play in contributing to, if not downright causing, your symptoms of anxiety and stress.

Clearly, inflammatory cytokines seem to play a significant role in activating and perpetuating the anxiety response. It would therefore seem prudent to address this part of the anxiety response in any treatment protocol.

In my opinion, not doing so would be like attempting to put out a roaring wildfire by pouring gasoline on top of it! In other words, we want to stop inflaming cytokines, not keep them inflamed.

How, then, do we begin to modulate some of these inflammatory substances? First, if you have signs and symptoms that could be indicative of an infection, then work with your physician and/or dentist to help identify which infection you might be suffering from and begin to appropriately treat that infection. Do not underestimate the power of simple physical maladies to wreak havoc on the anxiety response or increase your emotional stress.

This could range from a smoldering dental infection to an H. Pylori bacteria infection that causes ulcers to a bacterial or parasitic infection in the gut, to name just a few physical, treatable sources of your emotional response.

Also as important are the lifestyle modifications that you can make to improve inflammation, improve health and modulate anxiety. We will discuss several of those in this chapter:

## Laughter and Inflammation

Believe it or not, it *is* possible to laugh your way to a more balanced immune system and lower stress levels. A study measuring pro-inflammatory cytokines in patients with rheumatoid arthritis (a group known to have high inflammatory cytokine levels) compared to healthy individuals showed that the rheumatoid arthritis group had higher levels of cytokines such as IL-6 and TNF-alpha. Both groups were then asked to listen to a funny story before their levels of these particular cytokines were measured again.

The results showed that the levels of the pro-inflammatory substances were significantly reduced in the rheumatoid arthritis group, but remained primarily unchanged in the control group. Further supporting laughter's role in decreasing inflammation, and thus improving anxiety and well-being, was a study performed by researchers Dr. Lee Berk, MPH and Dr. Stanley Tan, MD.

These researchers divided diabetic patients into two groups. Both groups received standard medical treatment for their diabetes and cholesterol issues, but one group was assigned to watch 30 minutes of a program of their choice that induced a good belly laugh on a daily basis.

The study's participants were followed over the course of a year, making this a particularly valuable and long-range study of note. Markers of inflammation such as IL-6, TNF-alpha, INF-gamma and CRP were followed throughout that year, along with levels of HDL or "good" cholesterol.

The end result was that the patients assigned to the "laughter group" had a 66 percent drop in the levels of the inflammatory marker CRP, compared to a drop of only 26 percent in the non-laughter group. A significant decrease was also noted in the other cytokine levels and the levels of HDL or the "good cholesterol" increased as well.

Another study showed that laughter had the ability to reduce the levels of the stress hormones cortisol by as much as 39 percent and decrease adrenaline levels by as much as 70 percent, thus further reducing the negative impact that stress has on the body. So go ahead, a laugh a day may not only keep anxiety away, but perhaps keep the doctor away as well.

## Weight Loss and Inflammation

Next up in the lifestyle department, consider how your current body weight may contribute to your anxious symptoms. My suggestion is, if you are overweight, to start on a program to lose weight and gradually get you back on the path to good health. Not only will this be good for your overall health, but it will have a distinct and positive impact on your anxiety symptoms.

We talked earlier in this chapter about the hazards of inflammation and how that condition can exacerbate the stress response. Fat cells, or as they are known scientifically and clinically, adipocytes, have been shown to increase inflammatory cytokines such as IL-6 and TNF-alpha, the ones implicated in propelling the anxiety response.

In fact, a study published by the National Institute of Health in 2006 did show a significant link between obesity and an increased risk of anxiety and mood disorders. Another study published in no less than the *International Journal of Obesity* found obesity itself to be a risk factor for anxiety, independent of disease status or lifestyle factors. So, clearly, another potential benefit of weight loss is a proven reduction in anxiety symptoms.

So, where to start? Start somewhere. Our bodies were designed to move and many of my patients, anecdotally speaking, point to increased exercise as one way to improve their mood and reduce the symptoms of anxiety. I can't tell you which weight loss or exercise program is right for you, but I can tell you this: any program that you choose should focus on incorporating anti-inflammatory and anti-oxidant foods into your new lifestyle.

Foods high in omega-3 polyunsaturated fats have been shown to support a healthier response to stress and have also been shown to fight inflammation, which, as we've been discussing, greatly contributes to stress.

In fact, one animal study proved that offspring from a mother fed a diet deficient in omega-3 fatty acids had excessive response to stress later on in life. Another double-blind study done at Ohio State University looked specifically at 63 medical students; half were given 2.5 grams of omega-3 daily and the other half were given a placebo.

After a series of psychological tests and stressors, it was found that students who received omega-3 supplementation not only had less anxiety than their counterparts, but they also had less of the pro-inflammatory cytokine IL-6.

Finally, let's not ignore the old observation of "calories in, calories out." In particular, the caloric restriction that usually accompanies a lifestyle change and weight-reduction program has also been shown to significantly reduce inflammatory markers such as CRP.

Several studies suggest that significant decrease in CRP (up to 32 percent) can be achieved by reducing calories to 1,200 a day. It seems that caloric restriction itself is part of the mechanism by which a weight-loss program can reduce inflammation.

**Sleep and Inflammation**

Sleep is not only underrated, but often ignored by many adults as an integral part of stress and anxiety management. But, the fact is, getting enough sleep can improve your life all the way around, and not just when it comes to stress. Sleep provides many healing properties to the body, and helps to undo the damage done by the effects of a constant and unyielding anxiety response.

In fact, any weight-loss program should also focus on good sleeping habits as well. Part of developing good sleeping habits for a lifetime is knowing how many hours of sleep are required to keep you functioning optimally. The table on the next page can help you determine how much sleep you and your family need:

### Suggested Sleep Requirements

| Age (years) | Number of hours |
|---|---|
| 1-3 | 12-14 hours |
| 3-5 | 11-12 hours |
| 5-12 | 10-11 hours |
| 13-19 | 9 hours |
| Adults & Seniors | 7-8 hours |

**Figure 8.1:** *Suggested sleep requirements across a variety of developmental stages.*

Sleep and weight just naturally go together, and when your sleep is off balance, it can put your food choices (and, of course, your weight) off balance as well. According to UC Berkeley Sleep and Neuroimagining Laboratory, lack of sleep significantly impaired the function of the frontal (cognitive) lobe and this led to persistently poor food choices.

Specifically, these "poor food choices" tended to include refined, sugary foods known for their ability to not only increase inflammation but also contribute to poor blood sugar regulation, including bouts of hypoglycemia and elevated insulin levels.

Sleep deprivation also causes an increase in our hunger hormone ghrelin, thus driving us to eat not only more calories but more sugary foods as a way to quickly satisfy this "hunger." Of course, this only further exacerbates issues with weight gain and resulting inflammation. Studies show that lack of sleep can increase inflammatory markers such as IL-6 and TNF-alpha by as much as 40-60%.

Ever known that sluggish, lagging feeling after you don't get enough sleep? Then it should come as no surprise to you that sleep deprivation also decreases motivation and energy, causing us to be less active and only compounding the problem of weight plus inflammation.

Now, identify yourself in one of the sleep groups above and be honest about how many hours of sleep you get each night. This may require keeping a journal, as the less sleep we get, the foggier we tend to become. You may also find some patterns using this journal, such as the fact that you get a few more hours' sleep during the weekend than you do during the week, and what can you do about that?

Also, it may help us to identify our patterns of sleep disruption. Are you finding yourself falling into the 20 percent of Americans who get six hours or less of sleep nightly? If so, you may need to start taking steps to improve your sleep habits and reclaim your overall physical and mental health.

So, where should you start? The following are eight simple steps to improving not only the amount of sleep you get, but the quality of that sleep as well:

1. **Go to bed at the same time each night.** The body loves routine and it is critical when establishing new patterns and breaking old habits.

2. **Lose the soda, not the sleep.** Though it can be tempting, try not to drink caffeinated beverages after two in the afternoon, as they may keep you awake at night.

3. **Early to the gym, early to sleep.** Try not to exercise too close to bedtime, as this may cause all those hormones to float around your body, making it difficult for you to fall asleep.

4. **Have happy hour at an early hour.** It may seem like a nightcap or two will send you off to dreamland, but the fact is quite the opposite. Avoid alcohol use at night, as this may contribute to multiple awakenings during the night and difficulty going back to sleep.

5. **Create a relaxation routine prior to bedtime.** This may include relaxing baths, meditation, or even a cup of warm tea with decaffeinated herbs such as chamomile and lemon balm.

6. **Music to calm the savage beast.** Consider soothing nature sounds such as waves, wind, or even just relaxing music.

7. **Stimulation is the enemy of sleep.** When it is time for bed, be sure to turn off all lights, televisions, computers or any electronic equipment that can be potentially distracting or stimulating.

8. **If unable to fall asleep, get up and go outside and sit or read or pace until you get sleepy again.** Tossing and turning in bed is a great way to get preoccupied with lack of sleep, and even see your bedroom as a "bad" place. Designate the bedroom as your sanctuary for sleep and go elsewhere to get tired before you finally go "back to bed."

**Exercise and Inflammation**

What about exercise? What role does physical activity play in the increase, or decrease, of the anxiety response? Acute bouts of exercise have been shown to temporarily increase inflammatory markers. However, several small studies show that regular exercise actually *decreases* inflammation.

Individuals with stable congestive heart failure and intermittent claudication (pain on walking from poor circulation) showed a reduction in pro-inflammatory markers after 12 weeks and six months of regular aerobic activity, respectively.

Several markers of inflammation, such as CRP and TNF-alpha, decreased in marathon runners after nine months and healthy obese females after five months of regular activity. The average intensity used in these studies was aerobic activity for 30 to 45 minutes, three to five days a week. Clearly, the results weigh in the favor of regular exercise of a relatively moderate duration.

**Other Interventions**

What are other options to reduce inflammation and modulate anxiety? Well, we mentioned before that using Enbrel, an immune-suppressant medication used to treat autoimmune disorders, was shown to reduce pro-inflammatory cytokines and anxiety.

However, there might be significant side effects of this approach and the benefits may not outweigh the risks. Several studies have suggested that certain food supplements may help to modulate inflammation and be better tolerated. I include some of them here:

1. **Curcumin** (extract of Turmeric): The turmeric plant is part of the ginger family. The bright yellow, dried powdered version is commonly used as a spice in Middle Eastern and Caribbean Cuisine. Part of curcumin's mechanism of action is that of a potent anti-oxidant and anti-inflammatory agent. Several studies showed that turmeric did indeed reduce pro-inflammatory cytokines, as well as improve anxiety symptoms. One study even pointed to curcumin's ability to increase levels of neurotransmitters such as serotonin, dopamine and norepinephrine.

2.  **German Chamomile:** Chamomile was found in studies to have anti-inflammatory as well as mild anti-microbial (meaning the ability to kill bacteria) properties. In a randomized, double-blind placebo study (known as the "gold standard" of scientific research) involving 57 patients diagnosed with mild to moderate generalized anxiety disorder, chamomile was found to be effective in reducing symptoms of anxiety.

3.  **Resveratrol**: Several studies show that resveratrol, an extract from grapes, berries and red wine, reduces the pro-inflammatory cytokine TNF-alpha and IL-6, as well as other cytokines. These studies focused on resveratrol's ability to protect liver cells from damage generated by these cytokines. While I am not aware of any published study that specifically looked at resveratrol and anxiety together, there is one study that showed it reduced production of inflammatory cytokines produced by the glial cells. Remember that glial cells help to nourish and protect neurons as well as remove excess

glutamate from between cells, thereby preventing excessive stimulation of the excitatory NDMA receptors. There are many other studies elucidating resveratrol's role in preventing damage in the liver and kidneys from excess blood sugar levels, preventing and reducing risk of certain liver cancers by reducing inflammation, reducing inflammation in the lungs of smokers and protecting brain cells after traumatic brain injury. Earlier in this chapter we talked about the role of caloric restriction in reducing markers of inflammation. Well, it turns out that resveratrol's actions on the body can simulate the benefit of caloric restriction. Resveratrol seems to turn on the same beneficial gene that is activated by caloric restriction.

4. **Andrographis paniculata**: This is a bitter herb found primarily in India and Asia. It seems to be an immune modulator. In animal studies, it has been shown to reduce pro-inflammatory cytokines like IL-6 and TNF alpha, thus strengthening the immune system against infections and cancer. A randomized placebo study published in the *Journal*

*of Clinical Rheumatology* also suggests that it may play a role in improving symptoms of rheumatoid arthritis, another disorder with significantly elevated pro-inflammatory cytokines. **Warning:** Andrographis is recommended for short-term use only, and should not be taken if you have an autoimmune disorder.

**Case Study:** *Josh*

What about Josh? How were his symptoms progressing? What did his test results look like? And what form of treatment did I recommend? First, some test results: Josh's low hormonal levels, low serotonin levels, elevated CRP (a recognized marker for inflammation) and high cholesterol levels concerned me. And, when I explained what they meant, they concerned Josh as well!

We went over his dietary intake in detail and made a few minor adjustments that shifted his diet away from the typical American processed-, convenience- and fast-food way of eating and more toward the healthier Mediterranean style with its high anti-inflammatory fats, anti-inflammatory fresh herbs to season, and vegetables.

I also added a supplement that contained several anti-inflammatory herbs such as turmeric, resveratrol and milk thistle. We also started Coenzyme Q10, as Josh was on long-term statin use for his cholesterol. This nutrient has also been shown in studies to help decrease inflammation. Magnesium was also added to his regimen to replenish Josh's deficiency. Prior to adopting this regimen, Josh's blood pressure remained on the higher end, despite medications. Over the course of two months, however, we noted a gradual normalizing of his blood pressure.

I started Josh on testosterone-replacement therapy and an SSRI in the morning. Again, Josh's serotonin level was very low. Also, as his inflammatory marker was normalizing, I started L-Tryptophan at night since he was still experiencing difficulty sleeping. It worked very well and he felt like he was sleeping well for the first time in ages. He stated that his anxiety states had "completely resolved."

To add icing to the cake, Josh retired early and decided to spend at least the next few years "enjoying his newfound energy." I had to say that his treatments and therapy regimen had really paid off!

# Chapter 9:

## *Treat the Gut and Quiet Those Butterflies!*

I've talked at length about "the gut" in this book, and I'd like to revisit it now simply because research continues to support the theory that a healthy gut equals a healthy brain. We have already seen how manipulating the gut flora can lead to anxiety symptoms and mood disorders. So, it is clearly within reason to postulate that part of any healthy brain program needs to include a healthy gut program as well.

How do we determine if the gut is healthy? First, we must understand the basics of how the gut works so we can understand the potential triggers that can threaten the health of the gastrointestinal system.

As mentioned before, the gut contains about two-thirds of the body's immune system, millions of neurons, and is the primary site for the body's first interaction with the environment. It also controls the entrance of nutrients into our body. It lets us know when it is unhappy by producing symptoms such as bloating, gas, flatulence, abnormal stools (diarrhea or constipation), cramping and reflux. What's more, we are now discovering that the gut is a great indicator as to the presence of anxiety and mood disorders as well.

First and foremost, we tend to think of the gut as a digestive organ whose primary function is to digest and absorb food so that we get the nutrients we need to fuel us. Enzymes and other digestive juices are a big part of the digestive process and need to be present in sufficient amounts to ensure optimal nutrient extraction.

Enzymes are present in the saliva, the pancreas and, believe it or not, on the intestinal walls as well. We have Betaine HCL present in the stomach to keep the stomach at an acid PH so that it can continue the process of preparing the protein for continued degradation by the other enzymes.

Another important function of HCL acid is to sterilize the incoming food bolus (chewed and swallowed food). Without this process, one can get an overgrowth of yeast and bacteria in the gut that can cause dysfunction not just there, but throughout the entire body.

In the stomach there is a balance between the mucous-producing cells that protect the lining of the stomach from the acid produced by the parietal cells in the stomach. Oftentimes as we get older, however, this beautiful symphony can become disrupted and the lining of the stomach can become irritated or, worse yet, develop an ulcer. There are other things that can trigger this process such as stress, certain medications, foods and, yes, even bacteria.

In particular, the H. Pylori bacterium has been shown to damage the lining of the stomach. When the lining of the stomach is damaged, it becomes more permeable to particles of foods that can stimulate an immune response and inflammation.

If we recall from the previous chapter, inflammation is one of the major contributors to exacerbating the anxiety or stress response. When stomach acid is low, the overgrowth of bacteria that occurs can lead to production of toxins that can further irritate the gut, increase permeability and perpetuate inflammation.

A similar process can occur in the small intestine. The pancreatic and intestinal enzymes continue the digestive process. Insufficiency of these enzymes can lead to incompletely broken-down foods that can lead to gastrointestinal symptoms such as bloating, diarrhea and pain while also creating irritation and inflammation of the gut.

A comprehensive stool analysis can help to give some information about the gut. Specifically, it can provide vital information on the balance between "good" and "bad" bacteria, enzyme sufficiency, evaluate for markers of inflammation that may be associated with inflammatory bowel diseases or infectious bacteria and, if needed, the most appropriate treatment for pathogenic bacteria.

Food intolerances are another source of potential gut inflammation. Keep in mind that food intolerances are different from food allergies, as they are mediated by different parts of the immune system. Food allergies can present with hives, shortness of breath, wheezing and anaphylactic shock and, naturally, these foods should always be avoided.

Food intolerances, on the other hand, can contribute to a variety of symptoms that many times are not immediately associated with that particular food. A good example of this that also reveals how food can affect the brain is a condition referred to as "gluten ataxia." This is a condition that causes individuals to intermittently lose their balance. This can occur even if there is no evidence of inflammation in the bowels secondary to gluten. Fortunately, simply removing gluten from the diet improves this condition.

Another example of food intolerance is the ability of cow's milk to increase inflammatory markers such as the tumor necrosis factor alpha (TNF-alpha) in susceptible individuals. This pro-inflammatory cytokine has also been shown to stimulate the anxiety response. So as you can see, foods can have an adverse reaction on the immune system. Since a full two-thirds of the immune system is in the gut, it is easy to see how the gut can be irritated in a variety of ways, thus producing even more inflammation and increasing permeability.

It is important to be active in your own welfare, both physically and mentally. Learn what you can do and then do it. Case in point: part of your anxiety treatment may be to identify foods that could potentially be contributing to, or fueling, the anxiety response so that they can be removed from your diet.

How can you find out? There are several labs that perform food sensitivity evaluations including the ALCAT labs located in Fort Lauderdale, Florida. Another approach would be to undertake a food-elimination diet that removes foods that are more commonly associated with antigenic response, such as gluten and dairy. Other foods that have been implicated in an antigenic response are nuts, shellfish, eggs, soy and peanuts.

While this is an active form of treatment, it's not necessarily a speedy one. In fact, it may take four to six weeks before seeing any noticeable improvement in symptoms. A slow, systematic reintroduction of foods would then help to identify the foods associated with the symptomatology. Part of this plan would entail keeping a very detailed journal of symptoms, moods and foods to determine which are "fair game" and which to avoid.

If any agents of inflammation or infection have been identified, steps should be taken to remove them so that the healing can begin. Sometimes this requires treating with an antibiotic or an herbal remedy to remove the pathogen. Other times, as mentioned above, it may require removing the offending foods.

Another important treatment at this stage is the use of probiotics. Naturally, choosing a probiotic with a range of bacteria; including those that have been identified in studies to reduce anxiety, would be helpful. As you recall, two such anxiety-reducing probiotics, L. rhamnosus and B. longum, showed promising results in studies.

Not only will the probiotics potentially help mitigate the symptoms of anxiety, but they will also go a long way toward rebalancing the flora in the intestinal lumen. If the balance in the gut is shifted toward bacteria that produce byproducts that can potentially inactivate digestive enzymes, increase inflammatory cytokines and interfere with the production and processing of important vitamins, then this can adversely affect the health of the gut and thus the health of the brain.

If insufficient digestive enzymes or low stomach acid have been identified, you may want to replace them, as this would help to break down foods into the size optimal for digestion and help to avoid triggering of the immune system.

Here, too, it is important to eat foods that can promote a healthy GI tract, decrease inflammation and heal the intestinal mucosa (lining). For example, foods such as cranberries, garlic, broccoli sprouts and foods high in flavonoids have been shown to decrease inflammatory cytokines and even inhibit growth of pathological bacteria such as H. Pylori.

Other foods that can be beneficial to the body and reduce the precursors of anxiety are omega-3 essential fatty acid(s), which have been found to help reduce inflammation in the gut as well.

So, what's next? After offending substances have been removed, whether by an antibiotic, herbal antimicrobial or an elimination diet, then the next step is returning a balanced intestinal flora. This is done primarily by replenishing the so-called "good" bacteria and supplying the nutrients they need to grow and flourish.

Such nutrients are referred to as "prebiotics." Examples include FOS, soluble fiber and short-chain fatty acids. It turns out that the good bacteria require the same nutrients as us to survive, such as special sugars (FOS), carbohydrates (fiber) and special fats (short-chain fatty acids).

In this part of the treatment process it becomes important to take steps to repair the lining of the gastrointestinal tract. But, it can't be rushed and, in fact, the more you properly prepare for the treatment, the more successful the treatment will be.

That's because, interestingly, the essential amino acid glutamine is used in high amounts by the cells that line the gut to repair any damage. Certain pathogens such as yeast can also use glutamine to fuel their growth. Therefore, it is important to have a balanced flora prior to using glutamine as a tool for repair. Also, since glutamine can convert to glutamate, the excitatory neurotransmitter, it can exacerbate anxiety in susceptible individuals if levels are too high.

You won't have to go to the health food store for all your anxiety-reducing remedies, either. Simple, natural, easily obtainable foods such as bananas and okra can also go a long way to soothing symptoms by creating a mucous-type barrier to protect the gut's lining while repair is in progress.

For those seeking a slightly more "exotic" approach, slippery elm, derived from the bark of the tree for which it has been named, has been a time-honored approach used by Native Americans to soothe and coat an inflamed gastrointestinal tract. It is well tolerated and has a very good safety profile.

## Case Study: *Mary*

Mary's case was a little more complicated than either Josh's or Jennifer's. Specifically, she had had some major losses in her life and I felt that any approach we used for Mary needed to include some cognitive behavioral therapy as an adjunct.

Knowing the gravity of her situation, she agreed to do so. We also adjusted Mary's eating habits to include small, frequent meals. She felt too spent to exercise at this juncture, so we both agreed that we would have to address that topic after we got her feeling better.

When she came to see me, Mary had already been on a benzodiazepine for eight months, which meant it would require some weaning for her to undo her old treatment and begin a new regimen. We changed her prescription to one that had longer-lasting effects, so she would not have to take it as frequently, and began the weaning process.

I added an omega-3 supplement, as Mary was not eating well enough to obtain such nutrients from her diet. Her persistently elevated cortisol levels suggested that Mary's hypothalamic pituitary axis was in overdrive. To address this issue, I started her on a magnolia bark extract at night and asked that she incorporate massage therapy once a week.

As her progesterone level was low, I started Mary on a small dose of oral progesterone for its calming effects. Over the course of several weeks, Mary's sleep improved and she became much less anxious. Eventually, she was able to claim that she was sleeping "like a baby."

Treating her accompanying depression created more of a challenge. Her serotonin level was so low that I felt she would benefit more from therapy combining a medication with nutritional supplements. She had briefly tried L-Tryptophan in the past and experienced increased agitation.

My thought was it was most likely secondary to the gastrointestinal symptoms she was experiencing. We agreed to start an SSRI approved for anxiety and depression, along with magnesium and inositol, as they have been shown to augment the efficacy of cognitive behavioral therapy. Within a few weeks, Mary was starting to feel better.

Next, we had to address the gastrointestinal system in order to remove the fuel that was keeping the anxiety flame going. Evaluation of her stool revealed disproportionate bacteria flora with low probiotics and one potentially pathogenic bacterium.

We opted to treat with antibiotics with concomitant use of probiotic targeted to include the ones in the studies. We then incorporated digestive enzymes to help with digestion of proteins and fats.

Following the results of the food sensitivity test, we removed the foods from her diet that were challenging her immune system. We then embarked on repairing the gut with a medical food shake that included amino acids, glutamine and anti-inflammatory herbs such as turmeric, ginger and quercetin.

On follow up, Mary displayed evidence that she truly was a new person. Her moods had improved and she was starting to participate in her life again. Her therapy was going "great." Over the course of several months she was weaned off the benzodiazepine and tolerated that well. She was slowly increasing her exercise. We agreed to reevaluate her SSRI use after six to 12 months, and wean if indicated.

# Chapter 10:

## *Putting It All Together*

Living with chronic anxiety can be overwhelming and exhausting. It can leave us feeling edgy, irritable, and even lead to us gradually withdrawing from life because we can no longer handle any form of stimulation. It can decrease our productivity, deplete our finances and affect our relationships, leaving us feeling more isolated than ever.

But, you are not alone, and we are not at the end of learning how to treat anxiety. As the world becomes more challenging to live in, it is hopeful to note that more resources and research studies are being targeted to finding ways to manage this disorder while allowing us to be fully present in our lives.

Of course, there is anxiety and then there is Anxiety, with a capital "A." For those of you whose fear response has gotten so out of control that you legitimately fear that you won't be able to regain control, please know that there is hope. If nothing else, I hope this book encourages you to seek professional help from your physician or other qualified health care practitioner, as it is possible to return vibrancy to your life through treatment.

Don't go it alone; talk to people, research, study, reach out and get help. Too often we make assumptions that "no one will understand" or that "no one can help." People do understand and they can help, but not if you don't reach out and tell someone what is happening in your life.

Keep in mind that there are other disorders that can mimic anxiety as well, which is yet another reason to visit your physician. Self-diagnosis can seem easy and/or convenient, but when your health is on the line, don't you think you should consult a professional?

One thing everybody can do themselves is simply to assess your own situation and arm yourself with as much self-knowledge as possible before seeking treatment. The following checklist can help you to determine if you are actually anxious to begin with:

**A Checklist to Determine if You May be Anxious**

**Directions:** Circle, underline or place a check mark next to all of the symptoms that apply to you...

- Increased irritability

- You startle easily

- Difficulty concentrating

- Nausea when you think of anything "stressful"

- Butterflies in your stomach

- Sleep disturbances

- Increased tension in your muscles

- Constant worrying about everything and anything

- Feeling as if disaster is going to strike at any second

- Your heart is still racing long after you went to the mailbox expecting bad news and all you found was mail

- Palpitations

- Sweaty palms

- Feeling like you can't get a deep enough breath, but your speech is fine

- At its worse, shaking, sweating, breathing fast and feeling like things are closing in on you

**What to Do**

In a word; get help! Seriously. I cannot stress enough the importance of seeking medical attention immediately if you are experiencing symptoms of chest pain, palpitations, sweats and feeling dizzy. While these could be symptoms of a panic or anxiety disorder, it could also represent other serious issues such as heart attacks or abnormal heart rhythms.

Don't worry about such trivialities as cost or inconvenience, or ever be embarrassed for presenting with such symptoms. It is better to be safe than to ever worry about looking foolish.

So let's say you've regarded the list above, checked off a handful of items, ruled out – with the help of your physician – heart attacks, abnormal heart rhythms or other physical afflictions – and work from the point where other diseases have been ruled out and you have a diagnosis of anxiety.

The next step would be to find the root cause with the express desire to stamp it out. But first, we must isolate the cause. The following is a list that can help determine what is fueling your anxiety symptoms. Some or all of the following may be indicated:

1.) **Complete Blood Count**. Are you anemic? Even mild anemia can contribute toward anxiety. Women are more susceptible due to menstrual cycles and monthly blood loss.

2.) **Do you have a nutrient deficiency?** Not getting enough of a particular nutrient in your diet could be contributing to your anxiety:

- **Vitamin D**... can help to modulate HPA or stress axis

- **Vitamin B-12**... can help protect cells from damage

- **Magnesium**... can promote calming and help to improve efficacy of therapy

- **Folic acid**... is important in mental health and correlates with serotonin levels

- **Omega-3**... can help to maintain health and function of brain cells and decrease inflammation

- **Vitamin B-6**... helps with formation of calming neurotransmitter GABA and serotonin

- **Vitamin B-3**… has been shown in several case studies to have potential beneficial effect on relieving anxiety

3.) **Check Urine Organics.** This can be achieved through a diagnostic nutritional evaluation (see resources page for labs). Such a test…

- Can further elucidate functional deficiencies of nutrients
- Can indicate problems with bacterial imbalance in the gastrointestinal tract
- Can give an idea if the body is converting food into fuel efficiently
- Can give an idea if the body's detoxification system is functioning normally
- Can give an idea if the amino acid Tryptophan is being favorably metabolized or if there is an overproduction of its inflammatory components

**4.) Evaluate the Gastrointestinal System.** Check your gut.

Specifically:

- Look for balance between good bacteria and other bacteria
- Rule out bacteria or parasites that could be inflaming gut
- Evaluate markers of digestion and absorption
- Look for inflammatory markers that could suggest inflammatory bowel disease
- Look at levels of prebiotics or food for good bacteria

**5.) Evaluate Markers of Inflammation.** What might be causing your inflammation? Increasing it? Decreasing it? Contributing to it?

- High Sensitivity C-Reactive Protein- studies suggest that it correlates with increased levels of inflammatory cytokines
- Omega-3/Arachidonic Acid ratio- this is the anti-inflammatory/pro-inflammatory ratio. Also, high

234

levels of arachidonic acid may indicate overexcitation of neurons by excitatory neurotransmitter glutamate

**6.) Evaluate Hormone Levels.** Determine if your hormones are in balance and, if not, what is out of whack:

- Cortisol/ACTH- gives an idea of how the brain is communicating with the body during prolonged stress.

- Estrogen, Progesterone, Testosterone- especially around menopause and andropause (male equivalent to menopause). Deficiency or excess of these hormones can escalate anxiety symptoms.

- Thyroid hormone- an imbalance can lead to difficulty in managing anxiety symptoms.

**7.) Evaluate neurotransmitter levels-** (see resources page for lab)

- Serotonin - too little can lead to anxiety

- Norepinephrine - too much is anxiety provoking, too little can impair focus

- GABA - too little can lead to anxiety

- Glutamate - too much can drive anxiety response; too little can lead to memory issues

Depending on your results, you and your physician can determine if your anxiety can be managed with or without medication. Either way, there are things you can do before making that determination to begin addressing some of the potential physical causes for your stress response.

For instance, it is imperative that you start on a program to optimize your nutrition, as proper nutrition can enhance whatever modality you chose to implement. Regardless of how effective they may ultimately be, medication or herbal remedies can't take the place of proper nutrition.

The next step is to optimize your exercise program. Study after study continues to show the benefits of exercise for managing anxiety, depression, and memory; and, above all that, exercise is just all around a healthy brain and body intervention. It also helps to manage stress better on a longer-term basis. Remember to look beyond the stress of today to a brighter tomorrow, and focus on how building healthier habits can help both alleviate the stress you do have (today) and avoid future stress (tomorrow).

Other stress-management interventions such as meditation, massage therapy, essential oil therapy and biofeedback therapy (all of which were discussed earlier in this book) have all been shown to offer significant benefits. Cognitive behavioral therapy has also been shown as an effective tool for managing anxiety and helping individuals to implement strategies to maneuver successfully through their lives.

Finally, work on correcting any nutrient deficiencies that are identified, as they can sabotage the body's ability to replenish needed neurotransmitters and other substances.

# Bibliography

Abumaria, Nashat, and Inna Slutsky, Long-Jun Wu, Chao Huang, Ling Zhang, Bo Li, Xiang Zhao, Arvind Govindarajan, Ming-Gao Zhao, Min Zhuo, Susumu Tonegawa, Guosong Liu. "Enhancement of Learning and Memory by Elevating Brain Magnesium." Neuron, Volume 65, Issue 2. 2010.

Akhondzadeh S, Naghavi HR, Vazirian M, Shayeganpour A, Rashidi H, Khani M. Passionflower in the treatment of generalized anxiety: a pilot double-blind randomized controlled trial with oxazepam. 2001.

Allen RG., Bailey MT., Dowd SE., Galley JD., Hufnagle AR., Lyte M.. Exposure to a social stressor alters the structure of the intestinal microbiota: Implications for stressor-induced immunomodulation? Brain, Behavior, and Immunity. Ohio: Division of Oral Biology, College of Dentistry, The Ohio State University, 2011.

Bercik, Premysl, and Emmanuel Denou, Wendy Jackson, Jun Lu, Patricia Blennerhassett, Kathy McCoy, Elena F. Verdu, Stephen M. Collins. "The Intestinal Microbiota Determines Mouse Behavior and Brain BDNF Levels." Gastroenterology, Vol. 140, Issue 5.

Bravo, Javier A., and Paul Forsythe, Marianne V. Chew, Emily Escaravage, Hélène M. Savignac, Timothy G. Dinan, John Bienenstock, John F. Cryan. "Ingestion of Lactobacillus strain regulates emotional behavior and central GABA receptor expression in a mouse via the vagus nerve." Proceedings of the National Academy of Sciences, 2011.

"Bacterial Combinations Do Not Result In Enhanced Cytokine Production." World Journal of Gastroenterology, 2008.

Benjamin J., Frolov K., Fux M., Palatnik A.. "Double-blind, controlled, crossover trial of inositol versus fluvoxamine for the

treatment of panic disorder." Journal of Clinical
Psychopharmacology, 2001.

Barak Y., Belmaker RH., Elizur A., Gonzalves M., Kofman O.,
Levine J., Szor H.. "Double-blind, controlled trial of inositol
treatment of depression."American Journal of Psychiatry, 1995.

Bjelland I., Konstantinova S., Tell GS., Ueland PM., Vollset SE..
Choline in anxiety and depression: the Hordaland Health Study.
Norway: Department of Child and Adolescent Psychiatry, Haukeland
University Hospital, Am J Clin Nutr, 2009.

Blanco, C., Chou SP., Goldstein RB., Grant BF., Hasin DS., Huang
B., Saha TD., Smith S., Stinson FS. The epidemiology of social
anxiety disorder in the United States: results from the National
Epidemiologic Survey on Alcohol and Related Conditions.
Laboratory of Epidemiology and Biometry: J Clin Psychiatry, 2005.

Burton, Michael D, and Nathan L Sparkman and Rodney W Johnson.
"Inhibition of interleukin-6 trans-signaling in the brain facilitates
recovery from lipopolysaccharide-induced sickness behavior."
*Journal of Neuroinflammation*, 2011.

Boranić M., Gabrilovac J., Sabioncello A.. Psychoneuroimmunology-
-regulation of immunity at the systemic level. Zagreb: Immunological
Institute, 2008.

Boyer P. Do anxiety and depression have a common
pathophysiological mechanism? Paris 7 University: Acta Psychiatr
Scand Suppl., 2000.

Bush, David E. A., Erlich, Jeffrey C., and LeDoux, Joseph E..The role
of the lateral amygdala in the retrieval and maintenance of fear-
memories formed by repeated probabilistic reinforcement. New York:
Center for Neural Science, New York University, 2012.

Nemeroff, CB. The role of GABA in the pathophysiology and treatment of anxiety disorders. Department of Psychiatry and Behavioral Sciences: Psychopharmacol Bull, 2003.

Rothbaum, Barbara Olasov. "Critical Parameters for d-Cycloserine Enhancement of Cognitive-Behaviorial Therapy for Obsessive-Compulsive Disorder." *Am J Psychiatry, 2008.*

Fidecka S., Nowak G., Poleszak E., Wlaź P., and Wróbel A. NMDA/glutamate mechanism of magnesium-induced anxiolytic-like behavior in mice. Department of Pharmacology and Pharmacodynamics: Pharmacol Rep., 2008.

"EGb 761: ginkgo biloba extract, Ginkor." Drugs, R. D., 2003.

Maier, SF. Bi-directional immune-brain communication: Implications for understanding stress, pain, and cognition. Colorado: Department of Psychology and Center for Neuroscience, University of Colorado, 2003.

Ferencík M., Novák M., Rovenský J.. Relation and interactions between the immune and neuroendocrine systems. Bratislava: Institute of Immunology Faculty of Medicine, Comenius University in Bratislava. 1998

Kelley KW., Kooijman R., Weigent DA.. Protein hormones and immunity. Urbana: Laboratory of Integrative Immunophysiology, 2007.

Ferencík M., Stvrtinová V.. Is the immune system our sixth sense? Relation between the immune and neuroendocrine systems. Bratislava: Immunological Institute of Medicine, Comenius University, 2007.

Lepine, JP.. The epidemiology of anxiety disorders: prevalence and societal costs. Paris: Assistance Publique Hôpitaux de Paris, 2002.

Cronin MT., Hughes BM., Lynch L., Malone KM., O'Donovan A., O'Farrelly C., Slavich GM.. Clinical anxiety, cortisol and interleukin-6: evidence for specificity in emotion-biology relationships. 2010.

Flath B., and C. F. Jehn, D. M. Kühnhardt, K. Possinger. Plasma IL-6 and HPA-axis Function in Depression and Anxiety in Patients with Cancer. Journal of Clinical Oncology, 2005.

Haack M., Kraus T., Morag A., Pollmächer T., Reichenberg A., Schuld A., Yirmiya R.. Cytokine-associated emotional and cognitive disturbances in humans. 2001.

Harvey BH., Oosthuizen F., Wegener G.. Nitric oxide as inflammatory mediator in post-traumatic stress disorder (PTSD): evidence from an animal model. 2005.

Bremner, J. Douglas.Traumatic stress: effects on the brain. 2006.

Bercik P., Berger B., Bergonzelli GE., Park AJ., Blennerhassett PA., Collins SM., Deng Y., Fahnestock M., Huang X., Huizinga JD., Khoshdel A., Kunze W., Lu J., McLean PG., Moine D., Sinclair D., Verdu EF.. The anxiolytic effect of Bifidobacterium longum NCC3001 involves vagal pathways for gut-brain communication. 2011.

Bienenstock J., van der Kleij H., O'Mahony C., O'Mahony L., Shanahan F.. Protective effects of Lactobacillus rhamnosus [corrected] and Bifidobacterium infantis in murine models for colitis do not involve the vagus nerve. 2008.

Balamurugan R., Jayakanthan K., Nanda Kumar NS., Pulimood A., Pugazhendhi S., Ramakrishna BS.. Probiotic administration alters the gut flora and attenuates colitis in mice administered dextran sodium sulfate. 2008.

Bienenstock J., van der Kleij H., O'Mahony C., O'Mahony L., Shanahan F.. Loss of vagal anti-inflammatory effect: in vivo visualization and adoptive transfer. 2009.

Bercik P., Bergonzelli GE., Blennerhassett P., Cherbut C., Collins SM,. Corthesy-Theulaz I., Foster JA, Huang X., Jackson W., Khan WI., Lu J., Macri J., Potter M., Malinowski P., Neufeld KA., Verdu EF.. Chronic gastrointestinal inflammation induces anxiety-like behavior and alters central nervous system biochemistry in mice. 2010.

Burke HM, Epel ES,. Lerner GK., Mellon SH., Nelson JC., Reus VI., Rosser R., Shelly W., Wolf J., Wolkowitz OM.. Serum BDNF levels before treatment predict SSRI response in depression. 2011.
Cerdan J., Coudoré F., David DJ., Deltheil T., Gardier AM., Guiard BP., Guilloux JP., Hen R., Repérant C., Tanaka KF.. Behavioral and serotonergic consequences of decreasing or increasing hippocampus brain-derived neurotrophic factor protein levels in mice. 2008.

Jury J., McKay DM., Perdue MH., Sherman PM., Soderholm JD.,Yang PC.. Chronic psychological stress in rats induces intestinal sensitization to luminal antigens. Am J Pathol. 2005;168:104–114

Cardi E., Cavaliere M., Corrado G., Frediani T., Lucarelli S., Luzzi I., Pacchiarotti C, Rea P.. Positive association between Helicobacter pylori infection and food allergy in children. 1998.

Buret, Andre G.. How Stress Induces Intestinal Hypersensitivity. 2006.

Angel, Robert A., and Darin J. Knapp, Buddy A. Whitman, Tiffany A. Wills, David H. Overstreet, Hugh E. Criswell, Zhen Ming, and George R. Breese. Cytokine involvement in stress may depend on corticotrophin releasing factor to sensitize ethanol withdrawal anxiety. 2011.

Ascioti C., Audino MG., De Sarro GB., Masuda Y., Nistico G.. Behavioral and ECoG spectrum changes induced by incracerebral infusion of interferons and interleukin2 in rats are antagonized by naloxone. Neuropharmacology.1990.

Nistico G.. Communications among central nervous system, neuroendocrine and immune systems: interleukin2. 1993.

Dunn AJ., Smagin GN., Swiergiel AH.. Peripheral administration of interleukin1 increases extracellular concentrations of norepinephrine in rat hypothalamus: comparison with plasma corticosterone. 1996.

Krishnan RR., Lewis JG., Suarez EC.. The relation of severity of depressive symptoms to monocyte-associated proinflammatory cytokines and chemokines in apparently healthy men. 2003.

Krishnan RR., Lewis JG., Suarez EC., Young KH.. Enhanced expression of cytokines and chemokines by blood monocytes to in vitro lipopolysaccharide stimulation are associated with hostility and severity of depressive symptoms in healthy women. 2004.

Blom, Eva Henje. Pro-inflammatory cytokines are elevated in adolescent females with emotional disorders not treated with SSRIs." *Journal of Affective Disorders Volume* 136, Issue 3 , 2012.

Yirmiya R, Pollak Y, Morag M, Reichenberg A, Barak O, Avitsur R, Shavit Y, Ovadia H, Weidenfeld J, Morag A, Newman ME, Pollmächer T Illness. Cytokines, and depression. 2000.
Abe Y, Hashimoto S, Horie T.Curcumin inhibition of inflammatory cytokine production by human peripheral blood monocytes and alveolar macrophages. 1999.

Amanda M Gonzales and Robert A Orlando. Curcumin and resveratrol inhibit nuclear factor-kappaB-mediated cytokine expression in adipocytes. *Nutrition & Metabolism.* 2008.

M W Logue, C Baldwin, G Guffanti, E Melista, E J Wolf, A F Reardon, M Uddin, D Wildman, S Galea, K C Koenen, M W Miller. A genome-wide association study of post-traumatic stress disorder identifies the retinoid-related orphan receptor alpha (RORA) gene as a significant risk locus. Molecular Psychiatry. 2012.

Tim P. Moran, Danielle Taylor, Jason S. Moser. Sex moderates the relationship between worry and performance monitoring brain activity in undergraduates. International Journal of Psychophysiology. 2012.

Labuschagne I, Phan KL, Wood A, Angstadt M, Chua P, Heinrichs M, Stout JC, Nathan PJ. Oxytocin attenuates amygdala reactivity to fear in generalized social anxiety disorder. 2010.

Pum ME, Huston JP, Müller CP. The role of cortical serotonin in anxiety and locomotor activity in Wistar rats. 2009.

Yadav VK, Ryu JH, Suda N, Tanaka KF, Gingrich JA, Schütz G, Glorieux FH, Chiang CY, Zajac JD, Insogna KL, Mann JJ, Hen R, Ducy P, Karsenty G. "Lrp5 controls bone formation by inhibiting serotonin synthesis in the duodenum". 2008.

Montag C, Basten U, Stelzel C, Fiebach CJ, Reuter M. The BDNF Val66Met polymorphism and anxiety: support for animal knock-in studies from a genetic association study in humans. 2010.

Montag C, Reuter M, Newport B, Elger C, Weber B. The BDNF Val66Met polymorphism affects amygdala activity in response to emotional stimuli: evidence from a genetic imaging study. 2008.

Montag C, Weber B, Fliessbach K, Elger C, Reuter M.The BDNF Val66Met polymorphism impacts parahippocampal and amygdala volume in healthy humans: incremental support for a genetic risk factor for depression. 2009.

Kim H, Chen L, Lim G, Sung B, Wang S, McCabe MF, Rusanescu G, Yang L, Tian Y, Mao J. Brain indoleamine 2,3-dioxygenase contributes to the comorbidity of pain and depression. 2012.

Erhardt S, Olsson SK, Engberg G. Pharmacological manipulation of kynurenic acid: potential in the treatment of psychiatric disorders. 2009.
Oxenkrug GF. Tryptophan kynurenine metabolism as a common mediator of genetic and environmental impacts in major depressive disorder: the serotonin hypothesis revisited 40 years later. Department of Psychiatry, Tufts University School of Medicine and Tufts Medical,2010.

Melnikova NV. Neurokynurenines--seizures or/and anxiety in children with epilepsy? 2003.

Karpuzoglu-Sahin E, Hissong BD, Ansar Ahmed S. Interferon-gamma levels are upregulated by 17-beta-estradiol and diethylstilbestrol. 2001.

Shen Q, Lal R, Luellen BA, Earnheart JC, Andrews AM, Luscher B. gamma-Aminobutyric acid-type A receptor deficits cause hypothalamic-pituitary-adrenal axis hyperactivity and antidepressant drug sensitivity reminiscent of melancholic forms of depression. 2010.

Woelk H, Schläfke S. A multi-center, double-blind, randomised study of the Lavender oil preparation Silexan in comparison to Lorazepam for generalized anxiety disorder. 2010.

Chien LW, Cheng SL, Liu CF.The effect of lavender aromatherapy on autonomic nervous system in midlife women with insomnia. 2012.

Bradley BF, Starkey NJ, Brown SL, Lea RW. Anxiolytic effects of Lavandula angustifolia odour on the Mongolian gerbil elevated plus maze. 2007.

Pugh N, Ross SA, ElSohly HN, ElSohly MA, Pasco DS. Isolation of three high molecular weight polysaccharide preparations with potent immunostimulatory activity from Spirulina platensis, aphanizomenon flos-aquae and Chlorella pyrenoidosa. 2010.

Gertsch J, Schoop R, Kuenzle U, Suter A. Echinacea alkylamides modulate TNF-alpha gene expression via cannabinoid receptor CB2 and multiple signal transduction pathways. 2004.

Hart PH, Brand C, Carson CF, Riley TV, Prager RH, Finlay-Jones JJ. Terpinen-4-ol, the main component of the essential oil of Melaleuca alternifolia (tea tree oil), suppresses inflammatory mediator production by activated human monocytes. 2000.

Jae Yeon Chun, Ramakumar Tummala, Nagalakshmi Nadiminty, Wei Lou, Chengfei Liu, Joy Yang, Christopher P. Evans, Qinghua Zhou, and Allen C. Gao. Andrographolide, an Herbal Medicine, Inhibits Interleukin-6 Expression and Suppresses Prostate Cancer Cell Growth.

Xia YF, Ye BQ, Li YD, Wang JG, He XJ, Lin X, Yao X, Ma D, Slungaard A, Hebbel RP, Key NS, Geng JG. Andrographolide attenuates inflammation by inhibition of NF-kappa B activation through covalent modification of reduced cysteine. 2004.

Iruretagoyena MI, Tobar JA, González PA, Sepúlveda SE, Figueroa CA, Burgos RA, Hancke J. Andrographolide interferes with T cell activation and reduces experimental autoimmune encephalomyelitis in the mouse. 2005.

Amsterdam JD, Li Y, Soeller I, Rockwell K, Mao JJ, Shults J. A randomized, double-blind, placebo-controlled trial of oral Matricaria recutita (chamomile) extract therapy for generalized anxiety disorder. 2009.

Andreatini R, Sartori VA, Seabra ML, Leite JR. Effect of valepotriates (valerian extract) in generalized anxiety disorder: a randomized placebo-controlled pilot study. 2002.

Selective Interactions of Valeriana officinalis Extracts and Valerenic Acid with [H]Glutamate Binding to Rat Synaptic Membranes. 2011.

Lisa M. Del Valle-Mojica,* José M. Cordero-Hernández, Giselle González-Medina, Igmeris Ramos-Vélez, Nairimer Berríos-Cartagena, Bianca A. Torres-Hernández, and José G. Ortíz. Aqueous and Ethanolic Valeriana officinalis Extracts Change the Binding of Ligands to Glutamate Receptors. 2011.

Clive G. Ballard, John T. O'Brien, Katharina Reichelt, and Elaine K. Perry. Aromatherapy as a Safe and Effective Treatment for the Management of Agitation in Severe Dementia: The Results of a Double-Blind, Placebo-Controlled Trial. 2002.

Singh B, Singh D, Goel RK. Dual protective effect of Passiflora incarnata in epilepsy and associated post-ictal depression. 2012.

Srivastava JK, Pandey M, Gupta S.Del Valle-Mojica LM, Ayala-Marín YM, Ortiz-Sanchez CM, Torres-Hernández BA, Abdalla-Mukhaimer S, Ortiz JG. Chamomile, a novel and selective COX-2 inhibitor with anti-inflammatory activity. 2009.

Yi LT, Xu Q, Li YC, Yang L, Kong LD. Antidepressant-like synergism of extracts from magnolia bark and ginger rhizome alone and in combination in mice. 2009.

Emamghoreishi M., Talebianpour M.S. "Antidepressant effect of Melissa officinalis in the forced swimming test." *DARU* Vol. 17, No. 1, 2009.

Xu Q, Yi LT, Pan Y, Wang X, Li YC, Li JM, Wang CP, Kong LD.Antidepressant-like effects of the mixture of honokiol and magnolol from the barks of Magnolia officinalis in stressed rodents. 2008.

Lee J, Jung E, Park J, Jung K, Lee S, Hong S, Park J, Park E, Kim J, Park S, Park D.Anti-inflammatory effects of magnolol and honokiol are mediated through inhibition of the downstream pathway of MEKK-1 in NF-kappaB activation signaling. 2005.

Zhang M, Ning G, Shou C, Lu Y, Hong D, Zheng X. Inhibitory effect of jujuboside A on glutamate-mediated excitatory signal pathway in hippocampus. 2003.

Bradwejn J, Zhou Y, Koszycki D, Shlik J. A double-blind, placebo-controlled study on the effects of Gotu Kola (Centella asiatica) on acoustic startle response in healthy subjects. 2000.

Egashira N, Hayakawa K, Osajima M, Mishima K, Iwasaki K, Oishi R, Fujiwara M. Involvement of GABA(A) receptors in the neuroprotective effect of theanine on focal cerebral ischemia in mice. 2007.

Kakuda T. Neuroprotective effects of theanine and its preventive effects on cognitive dysfunction. 2011.

Anderson IM, Mortimore C. 5-HT and human anxiety. Evidence from studies using acute tryptophan depletion. 1999.

Miller HE, Deakin JF, Anderson IM. Effect of acute tryptophan depletion on CO2-induced anxiety in patients with panic disorder and normal volunteers. 2000.

Hudson C, Hudson S, MacKenzie J.Protein-source tryptophan as an efficacious treatment for social anxiety disorder: a pilot study. 2007.

Sarris J, Kavanagh DJ. Kava and St. John's Wort: current evidence for use in mood and anxiety disorders. 2009.

Sarris J, Kavanagh DJ, Byrne G, Bone KM, Adams J, Deed G. The Kava Anxiety Depression Spectrum Study (KADSS): a randomized, placebo-controlled crossover trial using an aqueous extract of Piper methysticum.

Pittler MH, Ernst E. Kava extract for treating anxiety. 2003.

Teschke R. Kava hepatotoxicity: pathogenetic aspects and prospective considerations. 2010.

Crocq L, Bugard P and Viaud P.. Fatigue Study Group inquiry into asthenia in general practice. Psychologie Medicale, 1978.

Crocq L, Bugard P et al., Treatment of astheno-depressive conditions by Minaprine-Multi-center study of 248 cases assessed by Fatigue Study Group Scale #4. Psychologie Medicale, 1980.

Dorman, T. et al. "The Effectiveness of Garum Amoricum (Stabilium) on Reducing Anxiety in College Students." *Journal of Advancement in Medicine,* Vol 8, 1995.

Pandaranandaka J, Poonyachoti S, Kalandakanond-Thongsong S. Anxiolytic property of estrogen related to the changes of the monoamine levels in various brain regions of ovariectomized rats. 2006.

Charoenphandhu J, Teerapornpuntakit J, Nuntapornsak A, Krishnamra N, Charoenphandhu N. Anxiety-like behaviors and expression of SERT and TPH in the dorsal raphé of estrogen- and fluoxetine-treated ovariectomized rats. 2011.

Hiroi R, McDevitt RA, Morcos PA, Clark MS, Neumaier JF. Overexpression or knockdown of rat tryptophan hyroxylase-2 has opposing effects on anxiety behavior in an estrogen-dependent manner. 2011.

Suzuki T, Sullivan DA. Estrogen stimulation of proinflammatory cytokine and matrix metalloproteinase gene expression in human corneal epithelial cells. 2005.

Janele D, Lang T, Capellino S, Cutolo M, Da Silva JA, Straub RH. Effects of testosterone, 17beta-estradiol, and downstream estrogens on cytokine secretion from human leukocytes in the presence and absence of cortisol. 2006.

Dovio A, Sartori ML, Masera RG, Racca S, Angeli A. Inhibitory effect of physiological concentrations of cortisol but not estradiol on interleukin (IL)-6 production by human osteoblast-like cell lines with different constitutive IL-6 expression. 2001.

Reumatismo. 2005 Apr-Jun;57(2):78-82.
[Effects of estrogen peripheral metabolism in rheumatoid arthritis]. [Article in Italian] Capellino S, Montagna P, Villaggio B, Cutolo M.

Schmidt M, Hartung R, Capellino S, Cutolo M, Pfeifer-Leeg A, Straub RH. Estrone/17beta-estradiol conversion to, and tumor necrosis factor inhibition by, estrogen metabolites in synovial cells of patients with rheumatoid arthritis and patients with osteoarthritis. 2009.

Cutolo M, Sulli A, Straub RH. Estrogen metabolism and autoimmunity. 2012.

Galeeva AY, Pivina SG, Tuohimaa P, Ordyan NE. Involvement of nuclear progesterone receptors in the formation of anxiety in female mice. 2007.

Baker ER, Best RG, Manfredi RL, Demers LM, Wolf GC. Efficacy of progesterone vaginal suppositories in alleviation of nervous symptoms in patients with premenstrual syndrome. 1995.

Galeeva AY, Pivina SG, Tuohimaa P, Ordyan NE. Involvement of nuclear progesterone receptors in the formation of anxiety in female mice. 2007.

Reddy DS, O'Malley BW, Rogawski MA Anxiolytic activity of progesterone in progesterone receptor knockout mice.

de Sarro, G.B., Bagetta, G., Ascioti, C., Libri, V. and Nisticò, G. "Microinfusion of clonidine and yohimbine into locus coeruleus alters EEG power spectrum: effects of aging and reversal by phosphatidylserine." *British Journal of Pharmacology*, 2005.

Cortese BM, Phan KL. The role of glutamate in anxiety and related disorders. 2005.

Curtis AL, Pavcovich LA, Valentino RJ. Long-term regulation of locus ceruleus sensitivity to corticotropin-releasing factor by swim stress. 1999.

Heyes MP, Saito K, Crowley JS, Davis LE, Demitrack MA, Der M, Dilling LA, Elia J, Kruesi MJ, Lackner A.. Quinolinic acid and kynurenine pathway metabolism in inflammatory and non-inflammatory neurological disease. 1992.

Eby GA., Eby KL.. "Rapid recovery from major depression using magnesium treatment". Medical hypotheses. 2006.

Eby GA., Eby KL. Magnesium for treatment-resistant depression: a review and hypothesis. 2010.

Toshiaki Kumea, Hanae Kouchiyamaa, Satoshi Kanekoa, Takehiko Maedaa, Shuji Kanekoa, Akinori Akaikea, , Shun Shimohamab, Takeshi Kiharab, Jun Kimurab, Kazuyo Wadac, Shinichi Koizumi. BDNF prevents NO mediated glutamate cytotoxicity in cultured cortical neurons. 1997.

Akinori Akaike, Yutaka Tamura, Yuko Sato, Takeharu Yokota. Protective effects of a vitamin $B_{12}$ analog, methylcobalamin, against glutamate cytotoxicity in cultured cortical neurons. *European Journal of Pharmacology,Volume 241, Issue 1*, 1993.

Gabriele Losi, Giulia Puia, Giorgio Garzon, Maria C. de Vuono, Mario Baraldi. "Apigenin modulates GABAergic and glutamatergic transmission in cultured cortical neurons" *European Journal of Pharmacology,* Volume 502, Issue 1, 2004.

Cohen SA, Müller WE. Age-related alterations of NMDA-receptor properties in the mouse forebrain: partial restoration by chronic phosphatidylserine treatment. 1992.

Liu HT, Hollmann MW, Liu WH, Hoenemann CW, Durieux ME.Modulation of NMDA receptor function by ketamine and magnesium: Part I. 2001.

Grenham S, Clarke G, Cryan JF, Dinan TG. Brain-gut-microbe communication in health and disease. 2011.

Nashat Abumaria, Bin Yin, Ling Zhang, Xiang-Yao Li, Tao Chen, Giannina Descalzi, Liangfang Zhao, Matae Ahn, Lin Luo, Chen Ran, Min Zhuo, and Guosong Liu, "Effects of Elevation of Brain Magnesium on Fear Conditioning, Fear Extinction, and Synaptic Plasticity in the Infralimbic Prefrontal Cortex and Lateral Amygdala." *The Journal of Neuroscience.* 2005.

Gilhotra N, Dhingra D. GABAergic and nitriergic modulation by curcumin for its antianxiety-like activity in mice. 2010.

Jithendra Chimakurthy, Murthy Talasila. Effects of curcumin on pentylenetetrazole-induced anxiety-like behaviors and associated changes in cognition and monoamine levels." *Psychology & Neuroscience*, Vol 3, No 2, 2010.

Sartori SB, Whittle N, Hetzenauer A, Singewald N. Magnesium deficiency induces anxiety and HPA axis dysregulation: modulation by therapeutic drug treatment. 2012.

Christine M. Albert, Claudia U. Chae, Kathryn M. Rexrode, JoAnn E. Manson, Ichiro Kawachi, Phobic Anxiety and Risk of Coronary Heart Disease and Sudden Cardiac Death Among Women: Circulation. 2005.

Anxiety and depression increase risk of sick leave. Norwegian Institute of Public Health, 2012.

Kathleen M. Thomas, PhD; Wayne C. Drevets, MD; Ronald E. Dahl, MD; Neal D. Ryan, MD; Boris Birmaher, MD; Clayton H. Eccard; David Axelson, MD; Paul J. Whalen, PhD; B. J. Casey, PhD. Amygdala Response to Fearful Faces in Anxious and Depressed Children. 2001.

David A. Morilak , Gabe Barrera, David J. Echevarria, April S. Garcia, Angelica Hernandez, Shuaike Ma, Corina O. Petre Role of brain norepinephrine in the behavioral response to stress Progress in Neuro-Psychopharmacology & Biological Psychiatry. 2005.

McEchron MD, Goletiani CJ, Alexander DN. Perinatal nutritional iron deficiency impairs noradrenergic-mediated synaptic efficacy in the CA1 area of rat hippocampus. 2010.

Coull JT. Pharmacological manipulations of the alpha 2-noradrenergic system. Effects on cognition. 2010.

Marowsky A, Fritschy JM, Vogt KE. Functional mapping of GABA A receptor subtypes in the amygdala. 2004.

Pláteník J, Kuramoto N, Yoneda Y. Molecular mechanisms associated with long-term consolidation of the NMDA signals. 2000.

Golan H, Grossman Y. Block of glutamate decarboxylase decreases GABAergic inhibition at the crayfish synapses: possible role of presynaptic metabotropic mechanisms. 1996.

Gouin JP, Carter S, Pournajafi-Nazarloo H, Glaser R, Malarkey WB, Loving TJ, Stowell J, and Kiecolt-Glaser JK. "Marital Behavior, Oxytocin, Vasopressin, and Wound Healing". *Psychoneuroendocrinology*, 2010.

Lisa E Goehler, Mark Lyte, and Ron P.A. Gaykema. Infection-induced viscerosensory signals from the gut enhance anxiety: implications for psychoneuroimmunology. 2007.

Giltay EJ, Enter D, Zitman FG, Penninx BW, van Pelt J, Spinhoven P, Roelofs K.Salivary testosterone: associations with depression, anxiety disorders, and antidepressant use in a large cohort study. 2012.

Vreeburg SA, Zitman FG, van Pelt J, Derijk RH, Verhagen JC, van Dyck R, Hoogendijk WJ, Smit JH, Penninx BW. Salivary cortisol levels in persons with and without different anxiety disorders. 2010.

Vinkers CH, Hendriksen H, van Oorschot R, Cook JM, Rallipalli S, Huang S, Millan MJ, Olivier B, Groenink L. Lifelong CRF overproduction is associated with altered gene expression and sensitivity of discrete GABA(A) and mGlu receptor subtypes. 2012.

Bülbül M, Babygirija R, Cerjak D, Yoshimoto S, Ludwig K, Takahashi T. Hypothalamic oxytocin attenuates CRF expression via GABA(A) receptors in rats. 2011.

Suwalska A, Lacka K, Lojko D, Rybakowski JK. Quality of life, depressive symptoms and anxiety in hyperthyroid patients. 2005.

Sait Gönen M, Kisakol G, Savas Cilli A, Dikbas O, Gungor K, Inal A, Kaya A. Assessment of anxiety in subclinical thyroid disorders. 2004.

Brady K, Randall C. Gender differences in substance use disorders. 1999.

Cognitive-behavioral therapy for adult anxiety disorders: a meta-analysis of randomized placebo-controlled trials. 2008.

Hunot V, Churchill R, Silva de Lima M, Teixeira V. Psychological therapies for generalised anxiety disorder. 2007.

Cognitive-behavioral therapy effective in combatting anxiety disorders, study suggests. Houston: University of Houston, 2012.

Schiller D, Monfils MH, Raio CM, Johnson DC, Ledoux JE, Phelps EA. Preventing the return of fear in humans using reconsolidation update mechanisms. 2010.

Matsumoto M, Togashi H, Konno K, Koseki H, Hirata R, Izumi T, Yamaguchi T, Yoshioka M. Early postnatal stress alters the extinction of context-dependent conditioned fear in adult rats. 2008.

Michael Davis. NMDA receptors and fear extinction: implications for cognitive behavioral therapy. 2011.

Licht CM, de Geus EJ, van Dyck R, Penninx BW. Association between anxiety disorders and heart rate variability in The Netherlands Study of Depression and Anxiety (NESDA). 2009.

Heart Rate VariabilityStandards of Measurement, Physiological Interpretation, and Clinical Use. 1996.

Heseker H. Psychological disorders as early symptoms of mild-moderate vitamin deficiency. 1992.

Möhler H. Nicotinamide is a brain constituent with benzodiazepine-like actions. 1979.

Velling DA, Dodick DW, Muir JJ. Sustained-release niacin for prevention of migraine headache. 2003.

Gerli S, Papaleo E, Ferrari A, Di Renzo GC. Randomized, double blind placebo-controlled trial: effects of myo-inositol on ovarian function and metabolic factors in women with PCOS. 2007.

Palatnik A, Frolov K, Fux M, Benjamin J. Double-blind, controlled, crossover trial of inositol versus fluvoxamine for the treatment of panic disorder. 2001.

Smith C, Hancock H, Blake-Mortimer J, Eckert K. A randomised comparative trial of yoga and relaxation to reduce stress and anxiety. 2007.

Janice K. Kiecolt-Glaser Martha A., Belury c , Rebecca Andridge d , William B. alarkey, Beom Seuk Hwang. Ronald Glaser. Omega-3 supplementation lowers inflammation in healthy middle-aged and older adults: A randomized controlled trial
Brain, Behavior, and Immunity. 2012.

Coppack SW. Pro-inflammatory cytokines and adipose tissue. 2001.

"Obesity Linked With Mood and Anxiety Disorder"
http://www.nimh.nih.gov/science-news/2006/obesity-linked-with-mood-and-anxiety-disorders.shtml Accessed 4/21/2013.

Zhao G, Ford ES, Dhingra S, Li C, Strine TW, Mokdad AH. Depression and anxiety among US adults: associations with body mass index. 2009.

Chen HF, Su HM. Exposure to a maternal n-3 fatty acid-deficient diet during brain development provokes excessive hypothalamic-pituitary-adrenal axis responses to stress and behavioral indices of depression and anxiety in male rat offspring later in life. 2012.

Yeh, Free. Release of C-Reactive Protein in Response to Inflammatory Cytokines by Human Adipocytes: Linking Obesity to Vascular Inflammation. 2005.

Janice K. Kiecolt-Glaser, Martha A. Belury, Rebecca Andridge, William B. Malarkey, Ronald Glaser. "Omega-3 supplementation lowers inflammation and anxiety in medical students: A randomized controlled trial". *Brain, Behavior, and Immunity,* Volume 25, Issue 8, 2011.

Mbimba T, Awale P, Bhatia D, Geldenhuys WJ, Darvesh AS, Carroll RT, Bishayee A. Alteration of hepatic proinflammatory cytokines is involved in the resveratrol-mediated chemoprevention of chemically-induced hepatocarcinogenesis. 2012.

Resveratrol attenuates hyperglycemia-mediated oxidative stress, proinflammatory cytokines and protects hepatocytes ultrastructure in streptozotocin-nicotinamide-induced experimental diabetic rats. 2010.

Xiaofeng Lu, Lili Ma, Lingfei Ruan, Yan Kong, Haiwei Mou, Zhijie Zhang, Zhijun Wang, Ji M Wang and Yingying Le. Resveratrol differentially modulates inflammatory responses of microglia and astrocytes Journal of Neuroinflammation. 2010.

Culpitt SV, Rogers DF, Fenwick PS, Shah P, De Matos C, Russell RE, Barnes PJ, Donnelly LE. Inhibition by red wine extract, resveratrol, of cytokine release by alveolar macrophages in COPD. 2003.

Burgos RA, Hancke JL, Bertoglio JC, Arriagada S, Calvo M. Efficacy of an Andrographis paniculata composition for the relief of rheumatoid arthritis symptoms: a prospective randomized placebo-controlled trial. Chile: Institute of Pharmacology and Morphophysiology, 2009.

Sheeja K, Kuttan G. Andrographis paniculata downregulates proinflammatory cytokine production and augments cell mediated immune response in metastatic tumor-bearing mice. 2010.

Sayyah M, Boostani H, Pakseresht S, Malayeri A. Comparison of Silybum marianum (L.) Gaertn. with fluoxetine in the treatment of Obsessive-Compulsive Disorder. 2010.

Messaoudi M, Lefranc-Millot C, Desor D, Demagny B, Bourdon L. Effects of a tryptic hydrolysate from bovine milk alphaS1-casein on hemodynamic responses in healthy human volunteers facing successive mental and physical stress situations. 2005.

Guesdon B, Messaoudi M, Lefranc-Millot C, Fromentin G, Tomé D, Even PC. A tryptic hydrolysate from bovine milk alphaS1-casein improves sleep in rats subjected to chronic mild stress. 2006.

Violle N, Messaoudi M, Lefranc-Millot C, Desor D, Nejdi A, Demagny B, Schroeder H. Ethological comparison of the effects of a bovine alpha s1-casein tryptic hydrolysate and diazepam on the behaviour of rats in two models of anxiety. 2006.

Buydens-Branchey L, Branchey M, Hibbeln JR. Associations between increases in plasma n-3 polyunsaturated fatty acids following supplementation and decreases in anger and anxiety in substance abusers. 2007.

Lazarewicz JW, Salinska E, Wroblewski JT. NMDA receptor-mediated arachidonic acid release in neurons: role in signal transduction and pathological aspects. 1992.

Volterra A, Trotti D, Racagni G. Glutamate uptake is inhibited by arachidonic acid and oxygen radicals via two distinct and additive mechanisms. 1994.

Naveilhan, P., Neveu, I., Baudet, C., Funakoshi, H., Wion, D., Brachet, P., and Metsis, M.. Dihydroxyvitamin D3 regulates the expression of the low-affinity neurotrophin receptor. 1997.

Obradovic D, Gronemeyer H, Lutz B, Rein T. Cross-talk of vitamin D and glucocorticoids in hippocampal cells. 2006.

Botez MI, Young SN, Bachevalier J, Gauthier S. Effect of folic acid and vitamin B12 deficiencies on 5-hydroxyindoleacetic acid in human cerebrospinal fluid. 1982.

Chubak J, Boudreau DM, Rulyak SJ, Mandelson MT. Colorectal cancer risk in relation to antidepressant medication use. 2011,

Xu W, Tamim H, Shapiro S, Stang MR, Collet JP. Use of antidepressants and risk of colorectal cancer: a nested case-control study. 2006.

Laverdure B, Boulenger JP. [Beta-blocking drugs and anxiety. A proven therapeutic value.] 1992.

Motrich RD, Gottero C, Rezzonico C, Rezzonico C, Riera CM, Rivero V. Cow's milk stimulated lymphocyte proliferation and TNFalpha secretion in hypersensitivity to cow's milk protein. 2003.

Hadjivassiliou M, Davies-Jones GA, Sanders DS, Grünewald RA. Dietary treatment of gluten ataxia. 2003.

Akbaraly TN, Brunner EJ, Ferrie JE, Marmot MG, Kivimaki M, Singh-Manoux A. Dietary pattern and depressive symptoms in middle age. 2009.

Liang W, Chikritzhs T. Affective disorders, anxiety disorders and the risk of alcohol dependence and misuse. 2011.

Lee SY, Shin YW, Hahm KB. Phytoceuticals: mighty but ignored weapons against Helicobacter pylori infection. 2008.

Halpern GM, Scott JR. Non-IgE antibody mediated mechanisms in food allergy. 1987.

James F. Flood, John E. Morley, and Eugene Roberts. "Pregnenolone sulfate enhances post-training memory processes when injected in very low doses into limbic system structures: The amygdala is by far the most sensitive." Vol. 92, 1995.

Brain Chemistry Ties Anxiety And Alcoholism. Chicago: University of Illinois at Chicago, 2008.

Zanardini R, Fontana A, Pagano R, Mazzaro E, Bergamasco F, Romagnosi G, Gennarelli M, Bocchio-Chiavetto L. Alterations of brain-derived neurotrophic factor serum levels in patients with alcohol dependence. 2011.

Carl Ernst, Andrea K. Olson, John P.J. Pinel, Raymond W. Lam, and Brian R. Christie. Antidepressant effects of exercise: Evidence for an adult-neurogenesis hypothesis? 2006.

Justin Rhodes. 'Good' Chemical, Neurons In Brain Elevated Among Exercise Addicts. Al Oregon Health & Science University, 2003.

Phongsuphap S, Pongsupap Y, Chandanamattha P, Lursinsap C. Changes in heart rate variability during concentration meditation. 2008.

Montano N, Porta A, Cogliati C, Costantino G, Tobaldini E, Casali KR, Iellamo F. Heart rate variability explored in the frequency domain: a tool to investigate the link between heart and behavior. 2009.

Williams LE, Bargh JA. Experiencing physical warmth promotes interpersonal warmth. 2008.

Kang Y, Williams LE, Clark MS, Gray JR, Bargh JA. Physical temperature effects on trust behavior: the role of insula. 2011.

Barry JA, Kuczmierczyk AR, Hardiman PJ. Anxiety and depression in polycystic ovary syndrome: a systematic review and meta-analysis. 2011.

Packer N, Pervaiz N, Hoffman-Goetz L. Does exercise protect from cognitive decline by altering brain cytokine and apoptotic protein levels? A systematic review of the literature. 2010.

T. Matsuzaki, A. Nakajima, S. Ishigami, M. Tanno and S. Yoshino. Mirthful laughter differentially affects serum pro- and anti-inflammatory cytokine levels depending on the level of disease activity in patients with rheumatoid arthritis. 2006.

Laughter Remains Good Medicine. American Physiological Society, 2009.

Field T, Hernandez-Reif M, Diego M, Schanberg S, Kuhn C. Cortisol decreases and serotonin and dopamine increase following massage therapy. 2005.

Michael Gitlin, Lori L. Altshuler, Mark A. Frye, Rita Suri, Emily L. Huynh, Lynn Fairbanks, Michael Bauer, and Stanley Korenman Peripheral thyroid hormones and response to selective serotonin reuptake inhibitors. 2004.

Ziccardi P, Nappo F, Giugliano G. Reduction of inflammatory cytokine concentrations and improvement of endothelial functions in obese women after weight loss over one year. 2002.

Heilbronn LK, NoakesM, Clifton PM. Energy restriction and weight loss on very-low-fat diets reduce C-reactive protein concentrations in obese, healthy women. 2001.

Lee C-K, Klopp R, Weindruch R, Prolla T. Gene expression profile of aging and its retardation by caloric restriction. 1999.

Larsen AI, Aukrust P, Aarsland T, Dickstein K. Effect of aerobic exercise training on plasma levels of tumor necrosis factor alpha in patients with heart failure. 2001.

Mattusch F, Dufaux B, Heine O, Mertens I, Rost R. Reduction of the plasma concentration of C-reactive protein following nine months of endurance training. 2000.

Tsukui S, Kanda T, Nara M, Nishino M, Kondo T, Kobayashi I. Moderate-intensity regular exercise decreases serum tumor necrosis factor-alpha andHbA1c levels in healthywomen. 2000.

Griffin ÉW, Mullally S, Foley C, Warmington SA, O'Mara SM, Kelly AM. Aerobic exercise improves hippocampal function and increases BDNF in the serum of young adult males. 2011.

Schmelzer C, Lindner I, Rimbach G, Niklowitz P, Menke T, Döring F. Functions of coenzyme Q10 in inflammation and gene expression. 2008.

Davidson RJ, Kabat-Zinn J, Schumacher J, Rosenkranz M, Muller D, Santorelli SF, Urbanowski F, Harrington A, Bonus K, Sheridan JF. Alterations in brain and immune function produced by mindfulness meditation. 2003.

Oman D, Hedberg J, Thoresen CE. Passage meditation reduces perceived stress in health professionals: a randomized, controlled trial. 2006.
Rainforth MV, Schneider RH, Nidich SI, Gaylord-King C, Salerno JW, Anderson JW. Stress reduction programs in patients with elevated blood pressure: a systematic review and meta-analysis. 2007.

Moonat S, Sakharkar AJ, Zhang H, Pandey SC. The role of amygdaloid brain-derived neurotrophic factor, activity-regulated cytoskeleton-associated protein and dendritic spines in anxiety and alcoholism. 2011.

Michael AJ, Krishnaswamy S, Mohamed J. An open label study of the use of EEG biofeedback using beta training to reduce anxiety for patients with cardiac events. 2005.

Ros T, Moseley MJ, Bloom PA, Benjamin L, Parkinson LA, Gruzelier JH. Optimizing microsurgical skills with EEG neurofeedback. 2009.

**Resources:**

**Laboratories:**

**Genova Diagnostics**- a fully accredited medical laboratory that offers a series of comprehensive nutritional evaluation. They also perform a comprehensive stool analysis
**Website:** http://www.gdx.net/

**Alcat World Wide**- CLIA certified lab that focuses on food sensitivity testing
**Website:** http://www.alcat.com/

**Metametrix**- a CLIA certified lab that focused on functional nutritional evaluation
**Website:** http://www.metametrix.com/

**Neuroscience labs- does n**eurotransmitter and immune testing
Website: https://www.neurorelief.com/index.php?p=home

**Food websites:**

www.skinnytaste.com- this website may be helpful for those undergoing a weight reduction program to get ideas on how to still make foods that taste good. It offers recipes with macronutrient values

**Books:**

**Live Younger in 8 Simple Steps by Eudene Harry MD-** Provides the foundation for healthy living at any age. Provides basic on hormones, nutrition, exercise role in supporting biochemistry of body

**Food your Miracle Medicine by Jean Carper-** one of the better referenced books on foods role as potent medicine that I have come across. Easy to follow

**Biofeedback Devices for Stress Management:**

**Emwave 2 by HeartMath technologies-** provides instant feedback utilizing heart rate and breathing to monitor how well doing with stress management program
Website: www.heartmath.com

**Resperate device-** this device has been shown in several studies to help with stress reduction and even reports some reduction in blood pressure readings with regular use
Website: www.resperate.com

**Exercise Your Brain:**

www.lumosity.com- This website offers mental exercises to improve brain health.  Stanford University recently did study that with consistent use it increases executive decision functioning

Made in the USA
Middletown, DE
31 October 2016